Charles Horetzky

Canada on the Pacific

Being an Account of a Journey from Edmonton to the Pacific...

Charles Horetzky

Canada on the Pacific
Being an Account of a Journey from Edmonton to the Pacific...

ISBN/EAN: 9783744756839

Printed in Europe, USA, Canada, Australia, Japan

Cover: Foto ©Andreas Hilbeck / pixelio.de

More available books at **www.hansebooks.com**

CANADA ON THE PACIFIC:

BEING AN ACCOUNT OF

A JOURNEY FROM EDMONTON TO THE PACIFIC
BY THE PEACE RIVER VALLEY

AND OF

A WINTER VOYAGE ALONG THE WESTERN COAST
OF THE DOMINION;

WITH

REMARKS ON THE PHYSICAL FEATURES OF THE
PACIFIC RAILWAY ROUTE AND NOTICES
OF THE INDIAN TRIBES OF
BRITISH COLUMBIA.

BY CHARLES HORETZKY.

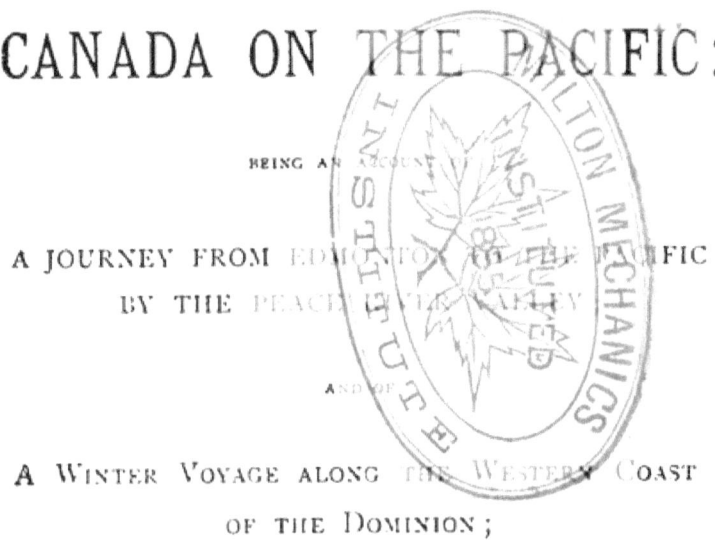

MONTREAL:
DAWSON BROTHERS, PUBLISHERS.
1874.

Entered according to Act of Parliament, in the year one thousand eight hundred and seventy-four, by DAWSON BROTHERS, in the Office of the Minister of Agriculture and Statistics of the Dominion of Canada.

TO THE

HON. ALEXANDER MACKENZIE,

PREMIER, AND MINISTER OF PUBLIC WORKS
OF THE DOMINION OF CANADA,

THE FOLLOWING PAGES ARE,

BY KIND PERMISSION, RESPECTFULLY DEDICATED

BY THE AUTHOR.

PREFACE.

THE following narrative comprises an account of a journey made to the Western Province of the Dominion, through a comparatively little known portion of the "Nor'-West" territory, and of a voyage along the whole Pacific coast of Canada.

The writer organized and conducted the overland expedition of Mr. Sandford Fleming, from Fort Garry to Edmonton, during the summer of 1872; and it was at the instance of that gentleman, who desired to exhaust the whole field of enquiry, before deciding upon a route for the Canada Pacific road, that the journey about to be described, was undertaken.

The Pine River Summit Lake Pass, referred to in this sketch, would also have been explored by me had time and circumstances permitted: but the period allotted for the journey, which included a visit to the river Skeena, compelled me to abandon the investigation of that locality. To the officers of the Hudson's Bay Company, without exception, the best thanks are due for the hearty welcome and aid extended to Mr. Macoun (my colleague), and myself, during our journey. To Lieutenant Ballantyne, late of H. M. S. *Sparrow-hawk*, and Capt. Lewis, of H. B. Co.'s steamer *Otter*, I am indebted for much valuable information regarding the harbours, and also the Indians of the British Columbian coast. Mr. Macoun, botanist, of Belleville, Ont., has also contributed very important data regarding the flora and growing capabilities of the Peace River country. In the section exhibited, from Lesser Slave Lake to the Fraser River, the reader will kindly bear in mind that absolute correctness is not to be expected. The elevations *may* be erroneous to the extent of one or two hundred feet; and I shall consider my deductions fortunate, if I am within a hundred feet of the truth. To those conversant with engineering technicalities and the fluctuations of atmospheric pressure, these remarks are of course unnecessary.

CHAS. HORETZKY.

OTTAWA, February, 1874.

CONTENTS.

CHAPTER I.

EDMONTON TO ASSINIBOINE.

The Start for Peace River—Object of the Tour—Outline of Intended Route—Confused and Discouraging Reports—Our Party—Dinner *al fresco*—How to Cook Pemmican—A Miscellaneous Cavalcade—Mackenzie River Watershed—Lake La Nonne—The Odometer—Fording the Pembina—Heavy Timber—Reach Fort Assiniboine 1

CHAPTER II.

ASSINIBOINE TO LESSER SLAVE LAKE.

Description of the Fort—A lazy Half-breed—The Clearwater—Chain of Swamps—Pack train Travelling—Rich Pasturage—Lesser Slave Lake—Skirting the Lake—The Traverse—Effective Shooting—Roman Catholic Missions in the North-West—Climate 16

CHAPTER III.

LESSER SLAVE LAKE TO DUNVEGAN.

A Delightful Country—The Grand Muskeg—Half-way to Peace River—Back into the Prairies—A Rude Awakening—Prairie Fire—A Cache—The Great Peace River Valley—Noble Landscape—A Grateful Surprise—Dunvegan 29

CHAPTER IV.

DUNVEGAN TO FORT ST. JOHN.

Farming Facilities—Minerals—Rare Field for the Geologist—The Grande Prairie—A Grizzly—More Sociable than Pleasant—Pine River—Burnt District—Indian Encampment—Route over the Rocky Mountains—Obstinacy of Indian Guides 41

CHAPTER V.

FORT ST. JOHN TO ROCKY MOUNTAIN PORTAGE.

Glimpse of Rocky Mountains—Portage Hill—Old Buffalo Tracks—Moose Steak—Mountain Terraces—A Stampede—Amateur Rafting—Rivière du Milieu—Hudson's Hope—Conversation under difficulties—Terrific Storm—Le Rapide qui ne parle pas... 52

CHAPTER VI.

ROCKY MOUNTAIN PORTAGE TO STEWART'S LAKE.

Past the Rocky Mountains—The Parsnip—Hardihood of Indian Voyageurs—A Mining Pioneer—Lake McLeod—First Winter Camp—Sagacious Dogs—Route of the Canada Pacific Railroad—Lake Stewart—Salmon—Fort St. James—Hudson Bay Company and North-West Discontent 65

CHAPTER VII.

STEWART'S LAKE TO HAZELTON.

Comfortless Encampment—Trout Fishing Extraordinary—The City of Hog'em—Frying Pan Pass—Lake Babine—Paddling for Life—Little Babine and Susqua—Invited to Christmas 83

CHAPTER VIII.

HAZELTON.

Physical Features—The Skeena—An Indian Ranche—Romantic Bridge—Curious Carving—Christmas at the Diggings

Contents.

—Up the Skeena—The Wotsonqua—A "Cholera Box"—
American Enterprise at fault—A hideous Cañon—Characteristics of Miners.. 102

CHAPTER IX.

HAZELTON TO NAAS.

Routes to the Coast—A Chinook Vocabulary useful—Skirting a Frozen River—Kitsigeuhle—Unpromising Quarters —A Greasy Caravan—Kitwangar Valley—Kitwancole—Pagan Orgies—Ingenious Carving—An Indian Mart—Lake Scenery — Welpamtoots — Valley of the Chean-howan—Trail lost —Muskeeboo—"Yorkshire" Indian—A Trying Walk—Naas Scenery—Alaska visible—Indian Suspension Bridge—Beyond the Chean-howan Cañon—Valuable Silver Lode—Basaltic Columns—A Native Bal Masqué—Kitawn. 113

CHAPTER X.

NAAS TO FORT SIMPSON.

Detained by Rain—Hazardous Canoeing—Camping on the Sea Coast—Geographical Outlines—Salmon Cove—Observatory Inlet—An Avalanche—Naas Harbour—South Inlet —A Critical Five Minutes—Work Channel — Chimsean Peninsula—Birnie Island—Arrival at Fort Simpson—The Harbour—American Military Post—Moral and Religious Condition of the Indians —Canoe Building—Agricultural Facilities 134

CHAPTER XI.

FORT SIMPSON TO NANAIMO.

On board the "Otter"—A "played-out" Boiler—Rose Spit —Graham Island—Masset Harbour — Clams — Mineral Wealth—A Nor'-Easter—Dundas Island—Fort Simpson again—Porcher Island—Arthur Channel—Seaforth—Bella Bella—Dean Channel—Bella Coula—The Old Route to Fraser River—Perilous Anchorage—King Island—Safety

Cove—Queen Charlotte Sound—Beaver Harbour—Description of Scenery—Discovery Passage—Alberni Canal—The Canada Pacific Route—Cape Mudge—Port Augusta—Off Nanaimo 152

CHAPTER XII.

Geology of Vancouver Island 169

CHAPTER XIII.

NANAIMO TO SAN FRANCISCO.

Nanaimo—San Juan—The Boundary Dispute—Victoria—Esquimault—Olympia—Opposition Stages—A Humiliating Break-down—Washington Territory—A Model Hotel—Reach Portland—On board the "Oriflamme"—Astoria—Arrival at San Francisco... 184

CHAPTER XIV.

The Canada Pacific Route 194

APPENDIX I.

The Indians of British Columbia 210

APPENDIX II.

On the Topography, Climate and Geology of the Western limit of the Fertile Belt, with some remarks upon the Rocky Mountains and the Peace River............................ 225

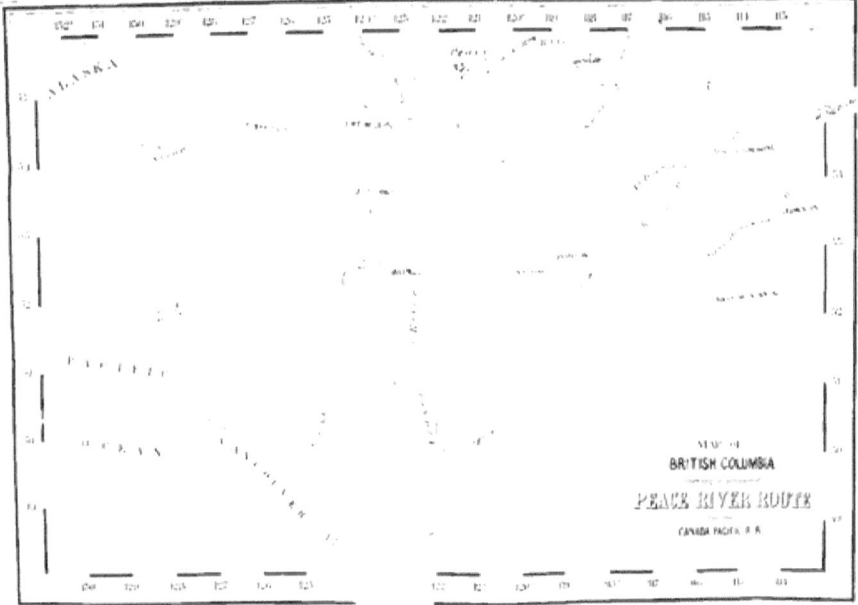

MAP OF
BRITISH COLUMBIA
PEACE RIVER ROUTE
CANADA PACIFIC R.R.

CHAPTER I.

EDMONTON TO ASSINIBOINE.

The Start for Peace River—Object of the Tour—Outline of Intended Route—Confused and Discouraging Reports—Our Party—Dinner *al fresco*—How to Cook Pemmican—A Miscellaneous Cavalcade—Mackenzie River Watershed—Lake La Nonne—The Odometer—Fording the Pembina—Heavy Timber—Reach Fort Assiniboine.

"HURRAH for the Peace River!" Such was the joyous exclamation of our botanist, as, after waving an affectionate adieu to our late travelling companions, he turned upon his heel, and remarked to me in a manner peculiarly his own, "Now *we* shall soon settle McLeod's theory."

It must here be remarked by way of explanation that in the early part of 1872 a pamphlet, styled "The Peace River," had been published in the city of Ottawa, setting forth the possibility of a line of communication between the Eastern and Western parts of the Dominion of Canada, by the Valley of the Peace River. The author of the article in question had, with great ingenuity, aided by extracts from an old Hudson's Bay Officer's Journal and

Diary, in imagination levelled up from the shores of Hudson's Bay to the summit of Peace River Pass, and after very closely (as will be shown during the course of this narrative) approximating to its elevation above the sea, urged the theory of a railroad from the Atlantic to the Pacific, by that route. The Chief Engineer of the Canadian Pacific road, struck by the possible advantages of such a highway, chose the writer of these notes to make a *reconnaissance* of that pass, and ascertain, as nearly as possible, its actual elevation. With this object in view, I left Edmonton in the beginning of September, 1872, accompanied by Dr. Macoun, an eminent botanist, *en route* for the Pacific coast.

Let the reader take up a good map of British Columbia, and thereon draw a line from Edmonton to Fort Assiniboine on the Athabasca ; thence, let him make a series of zigzag courses to the south-western extremity of Lesser Slave Lake, then north-westerly to the confluence of the Smoky River with the Great Peace ; from that point, in nearly a straight line, across the country lying north of that stream, to Dunvegan; next follow the Peace River through the Rocky Mountain Range to McLeod's Lake, and thence to Fort St. James on Lake Stewart, and he will have traced the first part of a very interesting journey,—interesting not only for its novelty, but also on account of the varied and magnificent scenery through which it was made.

Having, as already remarked, bade adieu to our late *compagnons de voyage*, and having seen them fairly under weigh for Jasper House, it now behoved me to make preparations for the Peace River journey, and as the season was already advanced no time was to be lost. A circumstance which lent an additional zest to our contemplated trip was the fact that we were in complete ignorance as to the proper means of procedure and the time necessary to accomplish the journey. Nobody at Edmonton could tell us aught regarding the Rocky Mountain Passes north of the Tete Jaune Cache. In vain did we seek for information as to our proposed journey. All the positive information we did obtain was that a Hudson Bay Company's boat annually descended the Peace River to the Rocky Mountain Portage, for the supply of leather required for the Indian trade in New Caledonia; but that boat had already been down and had long since returned to the west side of the mountains, and our chances of getting through to McLeod's Lake before the winter set in were very slim indeed. In fact, everybody was too willing to impart what knowledge he possessed, but as that was generally of a negative and contradictory character, we derived but little satisfaction or advantage from it. We were told by one party that such and such a route was not to be thought of; by another, that we might possibly make very slow and tedious progress on foot through the dense forests of the

Peace River, but that it would be folly to think of taking horses; and a third, and veritable Job's comforter, coolly affirmed that we would never be able to cross the "Grand Muskeg," which was described as infinitely worse than the famous dismal swamp of Virginia.

These conflicting and adverse statements, although rather disheartening, did not prevent my choice of some well-defined course, and I determined to strike across the country to Fort Assiniboine, and thence over the swampy and barren grounds intervening between it and the Lesser Slave Lake. But we had to bide our time. Two Hudson's Bay clerks, then at Edmonton, had received peremptory instructions from their superior officer at Fort Garry to immediately proceed to New Caledonia (a district of British Columbia) by the way of Peace River, and, as a matter of course, all the resources of Edmonton, in the way of horses, men and provisions, were laid under contribution in order to expedite their journey. This circumstance, coupled with the fact that Mr. Fleming had been supplied with the pick of men and horses for his trip to Jasper House, angured unfavourably for us, and added not a little to our anxiety. Notwithstanding those drawbacks, I set about making preparations for the journey as fast as it could be done under the circumstances; but little assistance, however, could be expected from the Company until Messrs. Y. and K. had been disposed of. On the 2nd of September those gentlemen's preparations being completed, they took their departure, kindly promising to smooth the way for us by leaving advice of our expected advent at every post they should pass; and, whilst bidding us farewell, adding that we should meet again only on the west side of the Rocky Mountains, as they would travel with customary Hudson's Bay celerity. The botanist, whose countenance during our affecting leave-taking of Messrs. Y. and K. had assumed a rueful and comically sad expression, especially upon their allusion to our keeping the rear all the way to Lake McLeod, remarked, after the last of the cavalcade had disappeared through the main gate of the fort, that "It was too bad to be left behind in this off-hand manner." "Never mind, my dear Mac.," said I; "we may not be so much behind them after all; and as they intend proceeding by canoe from Fort Assiniboine to Lesser Slave Lake, we may steal a march on them, and possibly get ahead of them yet."

The fact that provisions would not be readily obtainable when once away from Edmonton, until we reached Fort McLeod or the Omenica mines, rendered it imperative to carry supplies in quantity sufficient for a journey of nine weeks' duration. I accordingly packed up 230lbs. of flour, 12lbs. of tea, 24lbs. of sugar, and sundries, besides 150lbs. of pemmican (equal quantities of finely pounded dried buffalo meat and grease); meat and tea we expected to find at any of the solitary establishments of the Hudson's Bay Company which we might pass. Pack saddles and sundry horse trappings had to be made and fitted, men had to be chosen, and horses picked out from amongst the somewhat ill-conditioned animals left at the Company's horse-guard. In the meantime, Mr. Mac., who was to be my fellow traveller as far as Fort St. James, on Lake Stewart, whence he was to proceed to Quesnel and Victoria, busied himself in scouring the surrounding country in search of further botanical additions to his already bulky collection.

Our party, when ready, consisted of four persons, viz. :—the botanist, myself, and two hired men, one of them an English miner, named Robert Armstrong, recently arrived from the Omenica diggings on the Peace River, and who desired to return thither, having evidently failed to appreciate the society and advantages of the Upper Saskatchewan; the other, an English half-breed, by name Thomas, who turned out to be as lazy a rascal as ever munched pemmican. Of horses, we had six to pack and four to ride, making ten in all.

After many vexatious delays, Mr. Macoun, the two men, with nine horses and two carts (the latter I had decided to take as far as wheels could be made use of), left Edmonton on the 3rd of September, while I remained behind, intending to overtake them on the following day. My object in staying behind was to complete some barometric observations and settle accounts with Mr. Hardisty, whose kindness and hospitality had been unvarying. On the 4th, after breakfast and' saying "Good-bye" to the inmates of the Fort, I mounted my little nag, gained the high ground immediately behind the Fort, and taking a last look at the Saskatchewan, turned my horse's head towards Lake St. Albert, which I reached after a pleasant ride of nine miles. My first visit was to my old friend, Mr. Chastellain, who immediately saddled a horse, and expressed his intention of accompanying me for the first few miles towards Lake la Nonne. Before leaving, we paid a visit to his Lordship, Bishop Grandin, and the Oblat missionaries, who have a large establishment here. These gentlemen would not allow me to depart without partaking of some collation ; so we were detained until the forenoon was far advanced, and it was nearly eleven o'clock before we managed to escape from our kind friends. The day being fair, but cloudy, we rode along pleasantly for seven or eight miles, when Mr. Chastellain, after wishing all kinds of good luck to our expedition, turned his horse homewards, and I was left to pursue my way alone over the beautiful and undulating country.

At 1 p.m. I overtook our little train, which had stopped by the side of a small creek, and found the botanist and the two men busily and pleasantly employed preparing dinner. The preparation of this meal, and indeed of all our meals, which were unvarying in kind and quality, simply consisted in the pounding up with an axe of a couple of pounds of buffalo pemmican, which, after receiving an addition of water and a sprinkling of flour, was placed in a frying-pan, and heated. This mixture, together with tea and bread, was our daily food during the whole journey to McLeod's Lake, and, although very uninviting to a tyro, is the strongest food and the best for the traveller. One great advantage of pemmican is its portability. It can be compressed into very small bulk. A bag containing 100lbs. net weight measures but three feet in length by about ten inches in width, and will serve four men over a month. Our horses were quietly feeding on the rich and nutritious grass which lined the banks of the creek Those animals were of all shades of colour, and no two were alike in size. They were of the hardy little breed peculiar to the Saskatchewan country, and, though not much to look at, were possessed of qualities of endurance hardly to be expected from animals of their appearance. The horses, like the half-breeds of the country, understood a jargon, half French, half Cree Indian, and answered to such names as Bichon, Rouge, Noir, Sacré Diable, &c. I noticed with some concern, however, that one or two of them had a slight tendency to sore back, but Armstrong, the miner, had seen to them, and had, with great forethought, fitted relieving pads to the saddles.

Dinner being despatched, we saddled up again and resumed our journey. From Lake St. Albert to this point the land had been gradually rising westward, and we were approaching the dividing ridge between the waters of the Saskatchewan and those of the Mackenzie River. The character of the country was also beginning to change. Before dinner, prairie had prevailed over wood, but now the clumps of aspen and poplar became larger, and occurred more frequently, and the trees themselves began to assume a greater size. A few spruce trees appeared occasionally, and we saw that we were soon to leave the prairie behind us, at least for a time. As we left our dinner camp, a few drops of rain began to fall, and the clouds, which since morning had been gradually accumulating, being now surcharged, a steady rain set in, which continued without intermission until late the following morning. We had no alternative, however, but to go on, and we halted only at six o'clock by a fine lake of fresh water, having accomplished a distance of about thirty-four miles from Edmonton. After considerable trouble and delay we lighted a roaring fire, and, having pitched our tent, we proceeded to make ourselves comfortable for the night.

September 5th.—Still raining this morning, and in consequence we remained in camp until 9.30 a.m., when, the weather showing signs of improvement, we packed up and moved on through the woods in the direction of Lake la Nonne. Travelling this forenoon was particularly disagreeable, the long grass and bushes being laden with rain, and at every step, notwithstanding the utmost care, we received a perfect shower-bath. As we advanced, the trail began to change considerably for the worse, the ground becoming hilly and broken, and windfalls blocking up the road at frequent intervals. Several times during this forenoon's march we had to exert our united strength to extricate the carts from the many quagmires which we could not avoid, and at 1 p.m., when we stopped for an hour to rest our horses and boil our tea kettle, we had only made six miles by the odometer.

After dinner we resumed our march, the road becoming much worse, and in some places impassable for the carts, which, at every few yards, kept sinking up to the hubs. Two miles of this abominable road took us out into higher and drier ground, where the trail improved very much, and we were enabled to make satisfactory progress. We were now on the Mackenzie River Watershed, the small creeks flowing north-westerly and into the Athabasca. The height of land we had passed a little before dinner.

We arrived at Lake la Nonne before sundown, and camped close to Messrs. Y. and K., the two Hudson Bay gentlemen, who had only just arrived. They had experienced a great deal of trouble in passing over the last ten miles of ground, as indeed we had seen; the numerous freshly chopped windfalls we had passed testifying to the immense amount of road clearing they and their men had done for the general good. They were a little wroth at the idea of having pioneered for our benefit, and half jokingly, half seriously expressed the wish that we should take the lead next morning. "Well, gentlemen," said the botanist, "we started with the understanding that you were to go ahead, and keep ahead, and I only hope now that you will be men of your word, and do so still. Besides," continued he, "I thought you were fast travellers." Our two Hudson Bay friends being good-natured at bottom, took the taunting of our botanist in good part, and invited us to join them at supper, which we did, not having the patience to wait for our own. After sundown we strolled along the creek and lake margin in search of ducks and geese, which are very numerous about here.

Lake la Nonne is of small extent, and empties its surplus waters into the Pembina, the most southern of the prairie streams tributary to the Mackenzie River. It abounds with excellent white fish, and the surrounding country is thickly wooded. The soil is excellent, and from the general appearance of the country, not only here, but between this and Edmonton, we saw excellent opportunities for farming and stock raising.

The experiences of to-day not having impressed

us very favourably with regard to wheeled vehicles, I determined to abandon the two carts and pack our horses. The other party volunteering to try how far a cart could be taken, one of those rude Red River contrivances was handed over to them, with a request to keep the odometer register. For the information of those who have never seen anything of the kind, it may be explained that the odometer, or trochiameter, as it is sometimes called, is an instrument attached to the wheel of a vehicle, by which the number of revolutions is registered—this number, being multiplied into the circumference of the wheel, gives the distance travelled.—By 9 p.m. the camp was quiet, every one being pretty well tired out after the exertions of the day.

September 6th.—The morning broke bright and clear, and having breakfasted, we proceeded to pack the six animals picked out for that purpose, and moved off towards the Pembina by 8 a.m. A walk of an hour and fifty minutes brought us to the ford, where we found quite a large encampment of two or three white men, and some dozen half-breeds and Indians. Messrs. Y. and K., who had started before us this morning, had already arrived, and introduced us to Mr. McGillivray, another Hudson's Bay clerk, then on his way to Fort Edmonton. He had left Lesser Slave Lake some eight days before, and had come by boat through the lake, down the Little Slave River, and then up the Athabasca to Fort

Assiniboine, whence, to this point, he had journeyed by land. He described the trail as bad, and strongly advised our going from Fort Assiniboine by water; but, as I had already decided to proceed overland, he did the next best thing and secured to me the services of an English half-breed, named William Calder, and a most excellent man he afterwards turned out to be.

After partaking of Mr. McGillivray's hospitality, and thanking him for his kindness in forwarding our views, we separated, and forded the Pembina which is not more than a hundred yards wide at this point. The water was not deep, only taking the horses up to their bellies; but the bottom was of quicksand, and we needed to be cautious in picking our steps. We got over without accident, and a two hours' ride over a low and rolling country brought us to the Paddle River, on the bank of which our Hudson Bay friends decided to camp. At William's suggestion, however, we pushed on a mile further, and pitched our tent in the midst of a beautiful circular prairie, surrounded on all sides by thick woods. The next morning we were joined by the other party, and falling into Indian file, we proceeded rapidly on our way to the Athabasca. The country we passed through to-day was pretty level, and covered with dense timber, among which poplar, spruce and birch of large size predominated. Some of the spruce trees were of great size, and several we measured had a diameter of three feet. Wild fruits of different kinds were very abundant, such as raspberries, the service berry, and wild gooseberry, and we occasionally dismounted to pick and eat them to our heart's content. The botanist was in his glory, and made large and valuable additions to his stock. In point of numbers, our combined party had now assumed quite formidable dimensions, there being nine horsemen and twenty orses. Each man carried a shooting iron of some kind, excepting the botanist, who had, instead, a dilapidated tin case slung across his shoulder, which at every movement of his horse made row enough to frighten away whatever game there was in the vicinity.

We halted at noon to rest for an hour, as the weather was close and sultry, and our horses required careful handling to enable them to perform the long and difficult journey to Lesser Slave Lake. At half-past one we pushed on again, and reached Deep Creek, an affluent of the Athabasca, where we camped for the night. The Hudson Bay party proceeded on, intending to reach Fort Assiniboine that evening, if possible.

The next morning being Sunday, we did not hurry in getting away from camp, as we were within four or five miles of the Athabasca, and did not intend going further than Fort Assiniboine that day. It was, on this account, nearly nine o'clock before we were fairly under weigh. A steady drizzling rain was falling, and rendered travelling uncomfortable. In the course of two hours we reached the crossing place; but, owing to the late rain, the river had risen four feet, and we were compelled to follow up its banks for a mile or so, to where lay a large boat of the Company's, in which we crossed to the Fort, after driving our horses on to an island, whence they could easily be brought over during the afternoon. At two o'clock we landed at Fort Assiniboine.

CHAPTER II.

ASSINIBOINE TO LESSER SLAVE LAKE.

Description of the Fort—A lazy Half-breed—The Clearwater—Chain of Swamps—Pack train Travelling—Rich Pasturage—Lesser Slave Lake—Skirting the Lake—The Traverse—Effective Shooting—Roman Catholic Missions in the North-West—Climate.

THE valley of the Athabasca at Fort Assiniboine is large, and fully equal to that of the Saskatchewan at Edmonton. The river is larger and deeper than that stream, and 250 yards wide, with a very strong current. The so-called "Fort" is a mere collection of ruinous old log buildings, and is now used as a sort of half-way house between the two important posts of Lesser Slave Lake and Edmonton. We found one solitary clerk, who, with two or three Indians, were the only inhabitants of the place. Here we had intended to make some additions to our scanty stock of provisions; but the resources of the place being at the last ebb, nothing could be had but a few pounds of excellent butter, with which Mr. Calder, the resident clerk, kindly furnished us.

By odometer measurement, this place is about ninety miles from Edmonton, and two hundred and sixty miles from Jasper House, which is upon the same stream, but within the first range of the Rocky Mountains. Fort Assiniboine was, doubtless, in the good old days of the monopoly, a snug enough little spot; but it has been allowed to fall into decay. It is very nicely situated upon a fine level terrace about twenty-seven feet above the river. In the rear, the land rises to a considerable height, and is everywhere covered with thick forest; but the aspect was bleak and desolate in the extreme, and we felt glad that our stay here was to be of the shortest. In the course of the afternoon we made a tour of inspection, accompanied by Mr. Calder, who was heartily sick of the place, and intended leaving at the first opportunity.

Here we got rid of Thomas, the half-breed, and, paying him what was due, sent him back to Edmonton. He was a good-for-nothing fellow, and no loss to the party. William, who replaced him, undertook to pilot us across the barren grounds lying between this place and the Lesser Slave Lake. Accordingly, having overhauled our outfit, we prepared to start next morning.

September 9th.—Beautiful weather, and at 9 a.m. we started. Messrs. Y. and K. had left the day before by canoe, and expected to reach Lesser Slave Post in six days. However, the familiar French

B

proverb, "*L'homme propose mais Dieu dispose*," was well exemplified in their case, as they did not reach their destination until some time after us, much to the delight of Mr. Macoun, who did not forget our leave-taking at Edmonton, where they had so boastingly left us to bring up the rear.

The steep ascent from the Fort to the higher land tried our horses pretty well. We got up, however, without much trouble, and struck in a north-easterly direction, following a very old and indistinct Indian trail. The woods were very thick; and fire having passed through them in occasional spots, we experienced a good deal of difficulty in getting along. One or two of our refractory animals would not keep the trail, and, of course, came to grief the moment they set off on their own account. We travelled steadily until 4 p.m., when we reached a deep ravine, through which flowed the Clearwater, on its way towards the Athabasca. Having descended, and overcome the steep and soft banks on the opposite side, we camped, having made about fourteen miles over a perfectly worthless country. A good deal of the land we passed to-day was sandy, and supported the growth of a peculiar hardy pine, common in those regions, and known to the Hudson's Bay people as the cypress.

From the Clearwater to the Lesser Slave Lake occupied nine days; but the country was so uninteresting, our progress so slow, and the daily course of events so monotonous, that I shall pass over that interval. The intervening country bore a great resemblance to that lying between the head waters of the Ottawa and the southern shores of Hudson's Bay; being hilly, swampy, and densely wooded. The timber is principally spruce, balsam, poplar and birch; and wherever the land has any tendency to be level, it is almost invariably swampy, and covered with cranberries and blackberries. For nearly the entire distance, the trail was hardly discernible; our animals mired at every swamp we came to, and those were by no means of rare occurrence, the botanist having counted twenty-seven separate and distinct ones during the course of one day's travel. We seemed during those nine days to have experienced all the misfortunes incidental to pack train travelling. One of our horses was impaled on a sharp stump, and nearly bled to death; another, worn out by fatigue, ultimately became a prey to the wolves; our provisions got materially damaged; and, to crown all, the weather, which had been so propitious during our journey over the plains, seemed now bent on making us pay for former benefits, and enlivened us with continued storms of rain and wind, which occasionally alternated to sleet and snow. Upon the whole, we had a remarkable time of it, and were not sorry to catch the first glimpse of the Lake, which we reached on the afternoon of the 20th.

The last four miles before reaching the Lake were terribly hard upon the poor horses, the southern shore being for many miles a vast swamp, almost on a level with the water, and the soft ground sinking beneath us at every step. Indeed, by the time we got to a narrow strip of willows bordering a little creek, we were, one and all, glad to camp. The horses made up for their severe work by at once burying themselves up to the very necks in the tall and magnificent grasses which grow here in the greatest profusion. While putting up the tent, Armstrong shot a brace of geese which came tamely swimming down the creek, and failing to reach them from the bank, coolly plunged in, and swam for them.

After supper, we went to the mouth of the creek to choose a ford, and after an examination returned to camp and turned in.

Lesser Slave Lake is a very fine sheet of water, lying nearly due east and west, and about seventy-five miles long, by from five to ten miles in breadth. At the eastern extremity, its surplus waters find an outlet by the Lesser Slave River, through which, after a course of thirty or forty miles, they reach and mingle with those of the Athabasca. We had struck it about the middle, and our course now was to follow its margin, until we reached the Fort, situated at its western end. The waters of this lake teem with white fish *(coregonus albus)*, game in myriads frequent its shores, and can be easily got at in the numerous little nooks and bays. As a rule, the southern shores are low and swampy, while the northern side is higher, and often of a rocky nature. It is densely wooded on either side. Along this lake, then, we started next morning, but first had to effect the crossing of the creek, which delayed us considerably, the horses being much averse to the cold water, and requiring long and patient argument before we could induce them to take it.

The morning being raw and cold, it was decidedly unpleasant, after internally congratulating yourself on having got over the worst, to feel the animal beneath you suddenly sink in a hole, by which operation the waistcoat pockets were, in my case at least, filled with water. The creek, at our crossing place, was about thirty yards wide, and each rider before making the attempt, drew his knees up to his chin, fondly hoping in this position to be enabled to reach the other shore comparatively dry; but on nearing the middle, and sinking deeper and deeper in the cold element, that hope was rapidly dispelled, and the individual temperament of each member of the party was pretty well shown. Ejaculations such as "Oh! Gad!" and more powerful expletives, were heard, uttered in an ascending scale, and comically plaintive tone, as the ice-cold water gradually reached first over the boots, then filtered into the trouser pockets, and higher still in the case of the most unlucky ones. This diverting little prelude to the day's work having been gone through, we dismounted, and emptying our boots and ridding ourselves of the surplus water, resumed our way on foot, for the double reason of restoring the circulation and sparing our animals. The trail, when visible, which it very seldom was, sometimes led through the heavy "blue joint," and again through the woods, but always kept within a short distance of the shore.

At four in the afternoon we arrived at another creek, or rather river, as this was a large body of water, flowing with great rapidity, and requiring great care in fording it. After some delay, we managed to get to the other side, but not before the current had carried away an unfortunate but obstinate equine. The brute, regardless of yells, curses, and other arguments, marched deliberately into the worst place, and was, of course, whipt off his feet in the twinkling of an eye, and thrown bodily into the top of a large spruce which had been blown down, and now obstructed the river some few yards below. Reaching the unlucky animal, after some trouble, we succeeded in extricating him from his unfortunate position, and immediately turned our attention to camping for the night. After supper, much time was occupied in drying our wet packs and bedding, and it was not until ten that we were in a position to retire to our beds.

September 12th.—On calling the camp this morning,

I was surprised to see the ground covered with snow, and on looking at the thermometer, found the mercury at 31°. At eight o'clock we moved on, and in another hour were ploughing laboriously along the swampy margin of the lake. The soft ground was succeeded by occasional stretches of beach, covered with large round boulders, which, being coated with a thin film of ice, caused our poor unshod animals to slip at every step, and tried them very much. At three o'clock our progress was arrested by another good-sized creek, which we had to ford, and where the horses, losing bottom for a few yards, were obliged to swim. We camped at the other side. The next morning, a mile beyond camp, we encountered the third and last river, which we found impossible to cross in the usual manner; and after following it up for a considerable way, were compelled to cut down some dry spruce, and construct a raft, upon which, after driving over the horses, we conveyed our baggage and provisions.

This operation occasioned the loss of the forenoon, and after a six-mile ride through the most luxuriant blue-joint grass, we reached the "Traverse," just below Lesser Slave Lake Post, where we camped, and fired several shots, hoping that the reports might be heard at the Post, which, hidden from our view by a projecting point of land, lay about a mile and a half to the north-west; but we only succeeded in attracting the attention of two Indians who were hunting feathered game in the adjoining marshes. Those fellows were dressed in the unmistakable Hudson's Bay *capôt*, and were each armed with an old flint gun, with which they rather astonished our botanist. A flock of grey geese happening to pass a short distance, Mr. Mac. jokingly pointed to them, and, by signs, signified his desire to see them shoot. The two aborigines, motioning to us to keep quiet, immediately began to imitate the cackling of geese, and looking up, we saw the flock swerve slightly in their course and turn in our direction. When within shooting distance, although to our unpractised eyes they were yet too far, *bang, bang* went the guns, and a couple of plump geese fell into the grass beside us. These were a welcome addition to our larder, and proved a wholesome and palatable change from pemmican. A plug of tobacco a-piece in payment was received by the Indians with evident marks of pleasure, and they good-naturedly set to work to assist in collecting firewood and doing other little " chores " of the camp.

While we were sitting round the fire enjoying supper, one of the Indians, suddenly starting up, and pointing lakeward, exclaimed " sheman," and sure enough there were our two *ci-devant* fellow-travellers, the H. B. clerks, paddling up as hard as they could in the direction of the Post. We hailed them, and found they had been detained by hard winds and bad weather. They promised to send over a boat in the morning, so that we might put all our *impedimenta* across in one trip, and bidding us good night, passed on.

The following day we crossed over, leaving our horses to rest and feed at their leisure in the luxuriant pasture. The marshes in the vicinity of the Lesser Slave Lake Post are justly celebrated for the rich and unlimited quantities of wild grass, which grows in many places to a height of six feet, and is capable of affording feed for thousands of horses and cattle. The horses belonging to the establishment here always winter out, and in the spring are invariably found to be in the very best condition.

The post is situated on the north side of the lake, about forty feet above the lake level, which is something like 1,800 feet above that of the sea. It consists of some half-dozen ruinous old log houses, and is built in the form of a quadrangle. The Hudson Bay Company keeps here a resident clerk and some half-dozen men, who are generally either Indians or half-breeds. A small enclosure, containing a potato patch and some few turnips, beets, and carrots, was all we saw in the way of cultivating the soil, which is of excellent quality. The residents of the place depend upon the lake for fish *(coregonus albus)*, and rely chiefly upon game for their staple supply of food, a small and inadequate quantity of flour and groceries being annually imported from Edmonton, with the goods required for the Indian trade. This is gradually becoming less profitable every year, owing to the increased rate of mortality among the Indians, arising in some cases from actual starvation and the ravages of disease. The Indians of this locality, and indeed also those inhabiting the Peace River country, are quiet and inoffensive, and the white man may travel through their midst with perfect safety. In character and mode of living, they are totally unlike their brethren of the plains, who are occasionally of an aggressive disposition, and, as in the case of the Crees, treacherous, thievish, and confirmed liars.

The Roman Catholic missionaries have here a representative, a Mr. Remon, who, like his *confrères*, has sacrificed the advantages of civilized society to devote himself to the conversion of the Indians. This gentleman has built for himself a log shanty, which answers the double purpose of chapel and dwelling-house, and also serves as a school for the few native children at the place. He invited us to tea, and served us up a plentiful repast of third quality pemmican and tea, without the concomitants of sugar and cream. Indeed, from what the old gentleman remarked, I fear his superiors at Lac la Biche were a little remiss in supplying him with the actual necessaries of life, as his stock of provisions was exhausted. He told me he had not tasted flour for six months, so I, in return, asked him to our camp, where we treated him to the unusual luxury of fresh bread. He was very communicative, and gave me a letter of introduction to his *confrère* of Dunvegan, Monsieur Tissier. The society which furnishes the North-West Territory of Canada with missionaries of the Roman Catholic persuasion is an extraordinary one, and deserves, *en passant*, a tribute of respect and admiration for the self-sacrificing zeal, self-denial, and pluck with which each and every member, from their bishops down to the humblest lay brothers, prosecute the work of Christianization. They are bound by a vow of poverty, and they certainly carry it out to perfection, for they possess nothing but the clothes they actually stand in, whatever revenue they accumulate going to the Church and the maintenance of mission stations, the principal of which are at Lake St. Albert and Lac la Biche. The Mackenzie River and Isle à la Crosse districts possess the largest and most important of the Nor'-West stations, which are also the head-quarters of several bishops.

Although the vegetation in the vicinity of Lesser Slave Lake appears to suffer from the occurrence of early frosts, still, the belief of competent judges is that cereals could be successfully raised. At Lac la Biche, in about the same latitude, wheat culture has always been a success, and the Roman Catholic mission there annually supplies its outlying posts with that staple. The level country lying between Lesser Slave Lake and Lac la Biche supports a thick growth of timber, principally spruce and poplar, and the prevalence of "muskegs," or surface swamps, may account to a great extent for the summer frosts. Be this as it may, the country bordering on the North Saskatchewan, and also a portion of that adjacent to Manitoba, appears, from all accounts, to suffer fully as much from that drawback as this more northern region, which, therefore, must not be deemed, by reason of its higher latitude, unfitted to support a large population of emigrants. Indeed, the immense tract of country lying between Fort à la Corne and Lac la Biche seems to me to offer greater advantages for settlement than the open prairie situated to the south of the North Saskatchewan, where the cold is quite as severe as it is a couple or three degrees further North. The continuous belt of forest which forms the boundary of this northern section protects it in a great measure from the cold north winds which sweep the ocean of prairies situated to the south with irresistible violence, and render winter travelling dangerous and difficult in the extreme.

CHAPTER III.

LESSER SLAVE LAKE TO DUNVEGAN.

A Delightful Country—The Grand Muskeg—Half-way to Peace River—Back into the Prairies—A Rude Awakening—Prairie Fire—A Cache—The Great Peace River Valley—Noble Landscape—A Grateful Surprise—Dunvegan.

ON the 29th of September, having changed our Edmonton horses for a similar number of fresh animals, we took our departure from Lesser Slave Lake, our friends of the Hudson's Bay Company having preceded us by a couple of days. Mr. Mac. and the two men started one day ahead, while I remained behind, intending to overtake them at their second camp.

Bidding good-bye to Mr. Remon and Mrs. McGillivray, the wife of the gentleman we met at the Pembina River, who had treated us with the greatest kindness, I started early on the morning of the 28th, accompanied by an Indian lad. Our destination was now the Peace River, which we intended to touch at a point some sixty miles below Dunvegan, a post of the Hudson's Bay Company. Skirting the northwestern shore of the lake for several miles, we ascended a wooded ridge some three hundred feet above the level of the lake, and struck westward.

The trail being good, and the weather beautiful, we trotted along gaily, our horses' hoofs ringing upon the slightly frozen ground. The yellow leaves of the aspen and poplars strewed the path to a depth of several inches, and the aspect of the naked trees reminded me of the lateness of the season, and the necessity for speedy travel if we desired to pass through the Rocky Mountain range before winter set in. We travelled on through a very pretty country—now through woods, now over open grades, crossing an occasional tiny creek, and sometimes encountering a bit of swamp, which brought to my recollection our wretched trip from Fort Assiniboine; but we had evidently made a change for the better. We were passing over splendid soil, a rich light loam being its usual characteristic, and the timber of good size—truly, a delightful country to settle in. About two in the afternoon we reached the Grand Muskeg, the bugbear of this piece of road; but dismounting, and leading our horses over the hardest spots we could pick out, we made the firm ground on the other side without any trouble, and at six in the evening saw with pleasure the glimmering of the camp fire, which had just been lighted.

I calculated that we were now about half-way to

A Delightful Country.

the Peace River, having made about thirty-two miles from Lesser Slave Lake. My three fellow-travellers had got along without any difficulty, and had crossed the Grand Muskeg without being obliged to lighten the packs. The next morning we were all in motion at an early hour, and travelling in a north-westerly direction until eleven o'clock, we halted by a small creek, where we lighted a fire and rested for a time. The day was very fine, the thermometer standing at seventy-five degrees in the shade, while a warm southerly wind made the atmosphere quite oppressive; and after eating a hearty meal of pemmican and excellent smoked white fish, caught in the waters of Lesser Slave Lake, we felt more inclined to stretch ourselves on the grass and enjoy a long *siesta* than to resume our journey; but, as the botanist remarked, we were like that mysterious personage, the "Wandering Jew," and were condemned to go on.

A mile from our dinner camp we emerged from the woods, and entered upon a strip of prairie the surface of which was perfectly uniform, and almost a dead level, but with a slight downward tendency in a north-west direction. On our left, the creek beside which we had dined meandered alternately through woods and meadows on its way to join the Heart River, which we forded some eight or ten miles further on, and camped upon its banks. Since the forenoon the appearance of the country had undergone a remarkable change. Then our way lay through a dense forest of spruce and poplar, with occasionally some very fine larch in the swamps ; but now we seemed to be getting back into the prairies, and the landscape had much the appearance of the country between the second and third crossings of the White Mud River in Manitoba. The distance made good to-day we estimated at twenty-five miles.

30th September.—We were awakened this morning by finding our tent had gone by the board. A strong westerly gale was at its height, and the tent pegs having been carelessly driven into the ground the night before, a few strong gusts sufficed to disorganize the concern, and it required a considerable amount of ingenuity to extricate ourselves from the dismantled fabric.

At seven a.m. we were again on the march, and at nine o'clock had entered one of the thickest forests of poplars we had yet encountered. The trees, although of small size, grew so thickly together that any deviation from the beaten trail rendered advance impossible. Several times during the forenoon some of our most unruly pack animals branched off on their own account, and as often did they occasion us much trouble and delay in extricating them from the trees between which they got wedged, and where they, in one or two instances, tore away their packs. Towards eleven o'clock the weather, which had been threatening rain, cleared up, and we halted for dinner

Prairie Fire.

in a little open prairie. In lighting our fire, the grass, which was dry as tinder, caught, and in spite of our greatest efforts spread in a most alarming manner, and with almost inconceivable rapidity, but fortunately in the direction whence we had come.

By William's calculation, we were now within a very few miles of the Peace River; and the fact that the creeks were now flowing through deep gullies, showed us that we were approaching their outlets. Mr. Mac. and I, therefore, after hastily swallowing some hot tea, saddled up again and trotted on, leaving William and Armstrong to bring up the rear. The trail being well defined, we had no difficulty in finding our way through the woods, which were now of much heavier growth than those we had passed through in the forenoon. A short distance from our dinner place we came upon a quantity of moose meat, hung up out of the reach of the wolves, and killed, as we afterwards found, by an Indian who, upon our arrival at Slave Lake, had been sent to Dunvegan to acquaint Mr. Bourassa, the Hudson Bay agent there, with the circumstance of our being on the way. This *cache* had been made use of by our Hudson Bay friends, and, from appearances, they had helped themselves pretty largely. There still, however, remained sufficient for our use, and we proceeded to cut off and lay aside a choice piece for the men to take up when they passed.

Keeping on in a westerly direction, we crossed

one or two fine creeks flowing through deep gullies, and finally emerging from the thick woods into the open, we found ourselves upon the edge of a precipitous and grassy valley, at the bottom of which, and at a depth of fully six hundred feet, flowed the Heart River. Continuing along the plateau for a mile or so, another immense chasm opened out from the south, revealing another moderate-sized river, which joined the Heart immediately beneath us.

Quickening our pace to a hand-gallop, and lost in admiration of the landscape and the sudden transformation of the scene, we at length came to a dead stop on the brink of the Great Peace River Valley which now barred our progress westward. We had at length reached the long-looked-for goal of our hopes, and resting our nags for a little, we feasted our eyes on the glorious landscape now mapped out before us. Throwing the reins over our horses' necks, we let them feed for a few minutes, while awaiting the arrival of the others, who, with the pack animals, were still a mile or so behind. A strong westerly gale was blowing, but the air was so warm and balmy, that to recline on the beautiful grassy sward, full face to the blast, was positively delicious.

For several miles to the south-west, the noble river, flowing 800 feet beneath us, on its silent course to the Arctic Ocean, could be distinctly traced as it meandered through its mighty valley. Several large and wooded islands dotted its surface here and there, causing eddies and whirlpools, which in their turn made long and faint streaks of foam, barely visible in the distance. With the exception of these disturbing causes, the bosom of the mighty river was perfectly unruffled, and at our high altitude failed to convey an idea of the great velocity with which it flowed.

About a couple of miles to the south, the Smoky River, a very large tributary, mingles its waters with those of the Peace River. From our position, and embracing an angle of fully 150 degrees, or, in other words, from the North-west round to South, a boundless and nearly level expanse of country could be taken in at a glance, the only breaks being the great valleys of the Peace and Smoky Rivers, than which nothing we had ever seen could be more beautiful, the former especially, in its magnitude and depth, surpassing all we had anticipated. The width of the valley at this point cannot be less than two and a-half miles; and the banks, covered with verdure, and showing occasionally clumps of wood, slope downwards to the water edge in varied yet ever graceful form.

The arrival of the pack animals disturbed us in the silent contemplation of this wonderful scene; and the business of descending the steep slopes put a stop to any further reveries on the wonders of old mother Nature. In Indian file we followed the zig-zag trail, carefully leading our horses, and very speedily reached the lower terrace, after a descent which was accomplished by the horses in a half-sliding fashion, the sagacious brutes being wonderfully sure-footed, and exhibiting great 'cuteness in picking out the easiest and safest places.

Reaching the bed of the Heart River, we forded it with ease, and, a little further on, came upon the smouldering remains of a camp fire, close to which we found a note from our Hudson Bay friends, advising us of the correct state of their health, and that they had crossed—or rather were going to cross—the day before, at one p.m. Seeing no signs of their presence on the other side, we concluded they had done so in safety, and immediately set about the same operation ourselves; but, first, we had to find the canoe which usually served the purpose of ferry-boat. To our disgust and annoyance, after vainly examining the shore, we descried the much-coveted craft high and dry on the opposite bank. Bewailing our fate, we were about to construct a raft, when the report of a gun reached us, and a minute or so afterwards we saw, to our great surprise, a large boat under sail coming rapidly down the river. Upon our answering their signal, she altered her course, and headed right for us. She proved to be one of the Hudson Bay boats, belonging to Dunvegan, and had been sent to meet Messrs. Y. and K. This craft was manned by a motley crew of Indians and half-breeds, who understood nothing but French and Indian. They proved, however, to be a jolly set of fellows, and very willingly helped us to embark our baggage and provisions, which I now resolved to send up by this excellent and unlooked-for opportunity. The Indian who had been sent from Slave Lake was also on board, on his return thither, and I immediately arranged with him to take back the horses, reserving two for my own and William's use, as we determined on riding to Dunvegan, while the botanist, the miner, and the baggage were to go up in the boat.

Having by this time collected all our *matériel*, we crossed to the north side, and sent back two men in the canoe to pick out and drive over the animals we were to ride on the morrow. They had considerable trouble in separating them from the rest, the cunning brutes fully understanding the manœuvre intended; and it was only after much yelling and shouting that the men managed to get them into the water. When finally in, however, they swam for the other shore (550 yards distant), the men in the canoe encouraging them with yells and occasional taps from the paddles, while on the receding bank their equine friends regarded the proceeding with evident discomposure, and finally gave them a parting neigh, doubtless intended as a farewell. Immediately on landing, the animals were seized and mounted, barebacked and dripping as they emerged from their bath, and were at once treated to a hard gallop up and down the beach, to restore circulation; then a slight rub down, and they were busily engaged on the fine pasture in the midst of which we had pitched our tent.

By sundown the wind had lulled completely, and the sky was one glittering mass of stars; but the mercury was sinking rapidly, and by nine p.m. the thermometer stood at 29° Fahrenheit. The boatmen, however, were adepts at fire building, and had chopped enough wood to last an ordinary town household for a month; and we felt decidedly comfortable when, after supper, we sat or stretched around the huge fire, and listened to the Indians as they discussed matters in general, and our business in particular, and wondered what the deuce *we* could be after. Had we been Hudson Bay men, their wonder would have been at an end; but how two strangers should travel through the country without any apparent object, they could not understand.

The account they gave us of the state of affairs at Dunvegan was not very cheering. The New Caledonia boat had left three weeks before, and men willing to undertake the journey through the Rocky Mountains at this late season would be difficult to get. Having, however, had some experience of the mode of travel in the Indian country, and knowing how the class of men I had to deal with were given to over-estimate difficulties of the kind, I put no more questions, and dismissed the subject from my mind.

The morning of the 1st October dawned bright and cold, there being a sharp frost; but the sun gradually warmed up the atmosphere, and the day turned out beautiful. Breakfasting early, the boat, with its mixed freight, pushed off, and William and I saddled up, and providing ourselves with sufficient for dinner, mounted our ponies; and after winding up and down the slopes, now gaining the level of some fine terrace, now descending the banks of some tiny rivulet, finally gained the level of the country above, a height of eight hundred feet or thereabouts above the river.

The ascent had occupied nearly two hours; and as our direction had always been up stream, we found, on sweeping the horizon with the glass from our now exalted position, that the Smoky River was two or three miles below us. After a halt of five or ten minutes, we pushed on westwards over a prairie as level as those of Minnesota, and stopped for dinner on the edge of a lake. Two hours' rest, and we were again in the saddle. The uniformity in level had now slightly changed, but for the better, as the monotony of the prairie was broken by clumps or bluffs of timber, and the ground had changed from a dead level to an undulating roll, much more pleasing to the eye.

At five p.m. we rested at a small creek, and again setting off, and travelling for several hours in the dark, we descended the beautiful slopes immediately behind Dunvegan, and reached the Fort at nine p.m., having ridden about sixty miles since morning. Here we found Messrs. Y. and K., who had arrived four hours ahead of us. They informed me that, owing to the want of men and the lateness of the season, they had determined to return, or at least to cease the prosecution of the voyage westwards. They urged upon me the advisability of doing likewise, or of, at any rate, waiting until the winter set in, so that I might continue the journey on the ice; but I determined to go on, and, if absolutely necessary, to await the setting fast of the rivers either at Fort St. John or the Rocky Mountain Portage.

In the meantime, Mr. Bourassa had made preparations for supper, and very soon a smoking dish of moose steaks, flanked by a platter of very diminutive potatoes, was introduced, and ample justice was done to the repast by both William and myself. The absence of bread did not surprise me, as I knew that the Company only allow 100 lbs. of flour yearly to each clerk in this district, the freight upon even such a small quantity—coming, as it does, from Red River, *via* the roundabout Athabasca route—amounting to no inconsiderable item.

CHAPTER IV.

DUNVEGAN TO FORT ST. JOHN.

Farming Facilities—Minerals—Rare Field for the Geologist—The Grande Prairie—A Grizzly—More Sociable than Pleasant—Pine River—Burnt District—Indian Encampment—Route over the Rocky Mountains—Obstinacy of Indian Guides.

OWING to the fact that the Company's agents are liable to be suddenly removed from one post to another, those people are, not unnaturally, averse to the expenditure of the time and labour necessary for farming experiments; hence the absence of farm produce at these posts. But the natural advantages of excellent soil of unlimited extent, and the proverbially early disappearance of the snow in spring, would lead one to the belief that good crops of barley, potatoes, and fall wheat might be successfully raised in this part of the North-West.

Dunvegan, otherwise styled by the French "Fort de la Grande Prairie," owing to its proximity to the immense plain region lying some thirty miles to the south, and stretching from the Smoky River to the very slopes of the Rocky Mountains, is nicely situated upon a level terrace overhanging the silent waters of the Peace. Behind it, the ground rises to a height of seven hundred feet, and is chiefly of a prairie character. The Fort, a mere assemblage of some half-dozen log houses, is estimated to be one thousand feet above sea level; hence, the general elevation of the surrounding country is one thousand seven hundred feet, which is much the same as that of Lesser Slave Lake. The same elevation holds good on the south side, which is partially covered with a scattered growth of poplar and spruce trees.

The efflorescence of sulphate of soda is occasionally remarked along the slopes of the valley in the vicinity of Dunvegan, and cannel coal occurs within a dozen miles of the Fort, but on the south side. From the Rocky Mountain Portage to the Smoky River, a distance of probably two hundred and fifty miles, the Peace River, after taking a leap of two hundred and forty feet through the last and most eastern of the Rocky Mountain ranges, has cut its way through thick strata of clay and sandstone to a depth of seven hundred and eight hundred feet, where it flows over an almost horizontal stratum of limestone, which stretches northward as far as Lake Athabasca, where the primitive system meets the Silurian. The sections laid open to view by this river and its numerous tributaries offer an inviting field to the geologist, who might not find it difficult to show that the Peace River did, at some distant period, end its career at the spot where now it enters the plains, or, in other words, at the Rocky Mountain Portage, then a sea-washed rock, from which the waters gradually retiring, left it free to cut its way through the soft sea sands and detritus which form the comparatively level country over which the Beaver and other Indians now hunt.

On the 6th of October, Mr. K. left by boat for Fort Chipewayan, his fellow-traveller having previously set out on his return to Edmonton; and now having the coast clear, I arranged to proceed to Fort St. John with eight horses. I accordingly hired the services of a half-breed hunter, also an Indian lad to act as guide; and, accompanied by Armstrong, the miner, with whom I had already dissolved all connection, our party crossed the river, and started on our way for Fort St. John. At any other season of the year, the river route would have been easier and less expensive; but as my object was to see as much of the country as possible, I chose the former route, which, however (in order to avoid the rough and thickly-wooded country bordering on the Peace), promised to be a long and circuitous one.

Having swum our horses across, we ascended the banks on the southern side, and passing through several miles of rather open woods, we entered upon a rich and open country, and camped for the night about eight miles south-west of Dunvegan. The afternoon, although bright and clear, was cold enough to render a fire enjoyable; and our camp, thanks to our long-acquired experience in such matters, and under the influence of a cheerful blaze, soon assumed a very comfortable appearance.

A slight eminence in the vicinity enabled us to obtain a very fair view of the country to the southwest, which maintained its open character for many miles, until bounded by a rather high ridge of wooded hills lying nearly east and west, and on the other side of which was situated the " Grande Prairie." We observed that, curiously enough, the vegetation upon those uplands did not appear to have suffered so much from the effects of frost, this being probably due to the fact of the air in these upper regions being constantly in motion, while in the deep and capacious valley of the river the winds have often no effect.

The following morning, after breakfast, Mr. Macoun and I started off on foot, and in advance of the horses. We followed a well-defined Indian trail, which led us over the most charming country we had yet seen, passing sometimes through small poplars, but chiefly over an open rolling prairie land of the most excellent kind. We crossed numerous little creeks flowing northerly towards the deep *coulée*, which lay on our right, and at eleven o'clock we came suddenly upon a deep and precipitous ravine, about a quarter of a mile wide, at the bottom of which flowed a tiny rivulet. On reaching the bed of this little stream, the aneroids showed a difference of two hundred and eighty feet. A halt was called here; and while a fire was being lighted, we proceeded to examine the section exposed to view, which consisted of an immense layer of clay, sandstone, slate and fossiliferous limestone. Mixed up with these strata we found an excellent specimen of coal.

While wandering up the gloomy bed of the creek, a yell from the botanist startled us all, and his hurried re-appearance, minus hat and coat, with the information that he had seen a grizzly, started us off in pursuit of his bearship; but the unearthly howl of the botanist had evidently frightened him, as we could see nothing but some huge tracks leading up stream. A grizzly had undoubtedly been there, and, as Armstrong remarked, he must have been a "whopper." Mr. Macoun described him as being as large as a good-sized ox, and as having a most sinister expression of countenance.

After an hour's delay here, we ascended the opposite side, and pushed on through thick woods until five, p.m., when we camped. After supper this evening I tested the qualities of the coal we had picked up at noon, and found it to burn readily, giving a good, clear flame, with very little ash; the strong odour of real coal was emitted. We had, indeed, found a treasure; and when one reflects that hundreds of square miles of this beautiful country in all probability cover immense fields of this mineral, the future of this oasis in the great "Nor'-West" may be safely predicted.

October 11th.—" Weather still holding out fine and clear, with *cirri* from westward. On the march at seven, a.m., still travelling through the woods, and over a level country. Halted at noon as usual." Such were the jottings in the diary of this forenoon's march. We were not a mile from our last stopping-place when the barking of Indians' dogs caught our attention, and presently through the woods appeared, in single file, a family of Beaver Indians, on their way to Dunvegan, with fresh killed moose-meat, for barter at the Fort. They were the dirtiest, most ragged, and most powerfully smelling lot it had been our fate to meet, but from motives of policy I deemed it advisable to stop, though much against our wish. These filthy savages were all on horseback, and the women bestrode their ponies *en cavalier* like their better halves. They were wonderfully polite, and would not hear of our going any further that day. So we made a virtue of necessity, and after some consultation camped beside good running water. Our friends, the Indians, also came to anchor, and bothered us to trade for tobacco and sundry other articles, such as tea and ammunition. Mr. Macoun, chafing at the delay, started off through the woods to look for specimens, but a slight allusion to his grizzly-faced acquaintance of yesterday soon brought him back to camp. Those Beaver Indians are remarkably jealous of their wives, but are otherwise peaceably inclined, and passably honest.

The next morning we parted from our dusky friends and resumed our interrupted journey, which we continued until the 16th October, when we reached the Pine River, the largest tributary of the Peace from the Rocky Mountain Portage to the Smoky River.

The whole country passed over during those few days was varied in appearance, the trail passing through woods and prairie, principally the former, and for the last two days through a rough country covered with very dense forest. A good many large creeks were crossed, and they invariably flowed through deep depressions cut out by themselves, to a depth of three and four hundred feet, where we crossed them. Some very beautiful prairie land was also seen, but we always kept to the north of the "Grande Prairie," which, unfortunately, we had not time to visit; still the favourable appearance of the country we did pass through argued greatly in favour of the more southern section, about which we had heard so much.

On the afternoon of the 16th, and when yet a few miles south of the Pine River, we crossed an enormous tract of burnt country. The timber had been of large growth, principally spruce, and a luxuriant crop of grass had sprung up in the place of the burnt underbrush. The fallen trees formed a net-work very difficult to pass through, being, in some places, piled one on top of another to the height of six feet. For about a mile and a-half this *brûlé* very much retarded our progress. Finally emerging from the labyrinth of fallen trees, and gaining the summit of a high ridge covered with green timber, along which the path wound, we found ourselves upon the edge of a deep and gloomy ravine, leading in a northern direction, and evidently forming the bed of a small tributary of the Pine River, which we came upon as night began to enshroud the already gloomy landscape in its mantle of darkness. While skirting the edge of the deep gap already mentioned, we had caught occasional glimpses of the little stream flowing beneath at a depth of 1,000 feet. We were accordingly fully prepared for the precipitous descent which awaited us on gaining the edge of the Pine River Valley. The botanist and myself were some little distance a-head of the horses, and had passed the usual path leading down to the water's edge; so after waiting some time, we were not a little surprised to hear the voices of our men, far beneath and at the right of us. Not caring to retrace our steps, we plunged boldly down the precipitous banks, and rejoined the others after a descent which we most certainly would not have attempted in broad daylight.

On reaching the river's edge, we followed up the

gravelled bank, and camped opposite the fires of a large assemblage of Indians who were on their way to their fall hunting grounds. The deep and rapid river which separated our respective camps did not, however, prevent these gentry from crossing in their canoes to find out who we were, and otherwise gratify their curiosity, and hardly was our fire " under way," when we were surrounded by a crowd of chattering and inquisitive young braves, who were, otherwise, well enough behaved. Being unable to converse with each other to advantage, we contented ourselves with making arrangements for crossing in the morning, and retired to the enjoyment of a sound sleep, which we had fairly earned by our long day's march.

October 17th.—Our first care this morning was to seek out a secluded spot where we might enjoy the luxury of a thorough wash, and after breakfast, a young Indian placing his canoe at my disposal, I crossed to the other side. While making the traverse, I had an opportunity to observe the physical features of this singular locality. The stream was 150 yards in width, and flowed towards the Peace (only a mile distant) with a velocity of two or three miles per hour. Its deep and rugged valley could not be seen to advantage for any great distance upwards, but I believe it preserves its great size for forty or fifty miles, until it splits into several branches, one of which takes its source from a small lake situated on the summit of the main Rocky Mountain·Range.

Mr. Bourassa, of Dunvegan, had drawn my attention to the existence of this lake, and had so minutely described the peculiar physical features of this locality that I was strongly impressed with the idea that a very low and practicable pass in the mountains could be found there, the more so from the fact that another river, very inferior to the Pine in size, helped to discharge the waters of the same lake down the western slopes of the Rocky Mountains into the south branch of the Peace. While at Dunvegan, I had fully made up my mind to endeavour to cross the Rocky Mountain Range by that route, and had, with this object in view, been furnished with a letter addressed to an Indian thoroughly acquainted with the locality. This man, I had found out last night, was here on the very spot, and now formed one of the assemblage which stood on the other bank to await my arrival. On landing I speedily found out the man I wanted, whose name was M——, and showing him the letter, persuaded him to guide me at once to Fort St. John, some five or six miles distant. The horses we had hired at Dunvegan were still on the other side ; but Isidore, their owner, and the rest of the party, intended to follow me later in the day, and Mr. Macoun remained to superintend operations. A walk of one hour and a-half brought my Indian guide and myself to the Fort, which is built on the edge of an extensive alluvial flat, overlooking the Peace River. Here I found Mr. Kennedy, the clerk in charge, and having expressed my wish to cross the mountains by the Epinette River Pass, we soon had engaged the services of three other Indians, who, with M——, were to conduct me to McLeod's Lake by that route, while Mr. Macoun was to proceed by the river to the same point. But all my arrangements were soon broken through by one of my chosen band, a newly-married man, backing out, and his example being contagious decided the others to refuse, point blank, to proceed on the journey, which they now pronounced to be hazardous and difficult.

CHAPTER V.

FORT ST. JOHN TO ROCKY MOUNTAIN PORTAGE.

Glimpse of Rocky Mountains—Portage Hill—Old Buffalo Tracks—Moose Steak—Mountain Terraces—A Stampede—Amateur Rafting—Rivière du Milieu—Hudson's Hope—Conversation under difficulties—Terrific Storm—Le Rapide qui ne parle pas.

AFTER vainly essaying all manner of inducements, I had finally to give up the project, and take the only remaining alternative, which was to proceed to the Rocky Mountain Portage, and take our chance of finding a boat or canoe with which to ascend the river.

Several days being lost in getting men and horses for the trip, and collecting a large supply of fresh moose, pemmican, and other provisions, it was three o'clock in the afternoon of the 19th when Mr. Kennedy, William, two Indians and myself crossed the Peace River, with part of our baggage and seven horses, *en route* for the Rocky Mountain Portage, distant some fifty miles. The stream being three hundred yards wide, with a very strong current, the usual difficulty and loss of time was experienced in getting the horses across. While the men were fitting on the packs and saddling up, I shouldered my rifle and gained the high ground above, after a steep and laborious ascent of twenty-five minutes. The aneroids gave a difference of level amounting to eight hundred and sixteen feet above the water, and from this elevated position a most beautiful view of the country was obtained. Immediately beneath, and at my very feet, lay the little fort, the doors and windows being just discernible in the distance, while behind it, to the south, the high ridge of the right bank of the Pine River could be traced for many miles to the south-west. The whole country in that direction was one mass of dense forest, extending right up to the outer and most eastern range of the Rocky Mountains, which were distinctly visible. Away in the farther distance, a few snow-capped and isolated peaks, of the higher range, reared their serrated summits high in the clear and cloudless sky, and, owing to a peculiar state of the atmosphere, seemed to vibrate and tremble as each successive ray of the now rapidly declining sun impinged upon their snowy sides. A conspicuous mountain, of moderate height (called the Portage Hill), bore north $107°$ west, allowing $25°$ easterly variation, and formed a pretty and conspicuous landmark in the distance.

The appearance of Mr. Kennedy with the horses

caused me to abandon the delightful prospect, and taking a last look at the fort and river, I saw two "dug-outs" (canoes) pushing off with Mr. Macoun and the rest of the baggage. "They have a strong current against them all the way to the portage," said Mr. Kennedy, "and you need not look for them there before three days." Mounting a nag which Mr. Kennedy had kindly provided for me, we broke into a smart canter, following a level and well-worn trail, which took us through alternate copses of poplars and prairie. For six miles we kept on, and camped in a lovely spot in the midst of some fine trees. While sitting round our cheerful camp fire, Mr. Kennedy beguiled the time with stories and interesting information bearing upon the locality. "Just where you got into the saddle," said he, "two years ago, a big buffalo bull got his death wound. He must have strayed far from his comrades." "But," I asked, "where were his comrades? he surely never swam the river." "Oh," said Kennedy, "there are still some stray bands away north of us, and they are even yet seen occasionally at Rivière Salee, quite close to Lake Athabasca." In fact, the old buffalo trails are still distinctly visible on the grassy slopes opposite the fort, and it must have been a glorious sight when, in the old times, numerous bands, led by some huge bull with shaggy mane, might have been seen winding down the valley sides to slake their thirst in the cool waters of the Peace. Alas, for the poor

Indians! those happy days have passed away, and in a few years more not a bison will be left, and their whitened skulls and well-marked roads will be the sole vestiges of a once numerous and magnificent species. The moose deer, also bears, black, grizzly, and cinnamon-coloured, are still very numerous on the Peace River. The day we left the fort, a huge brute of the grizzly kind was shot quite close to the house. The annual slaughter of bears of various kinds on the Peace River is about four hundred, while almost fabulous quantities of moose meat are annually consumed at the different posts of the Company upon this river; but the reckless slaughter of wild animals habitually indulged in by the Indians and half-bred Iroquois trappers of the Smoky River, will surely bring its own retribution; and some years hence the Indians will be obliged to resort to other means of livelihood than the chase.

Sunday, 20th October.—A sharp frost this morning made us glad to huddle around the fire, but the day promising to be fine, we packed up and were on our way at an early hour, after breakfasting on delicious moose-steaks fried in onions, a plentiful supply of the latter having been kindly furnished by Mr. Kennedy, who has a very fine garden at Fort St. John, where his vegetables are equal to any that can be seen in the eastern markets. At 10.45, a.m., we came to a deep ravine, through which a small river from the north entered the Peace. This gully was fully 800 feet deep, and the descent and the ascent on the other side were very laborious. Half-a-mile below we could discern our two canoes paddling up stream, and from our great elevation their occupants seemed about the size of crows. Gaining the top of a fine level terrace, fully three miles in length, we put our horses to a gallop, and brought up at the end, where we halted for dinner.

During the interval I photographed the river, which struck me as being very beautiful at this place. On our right, high sandstone bluffs, hidden by a superficial layer of soil, rose to a great altitude, their summits being fully one thousand feet above the river. This forenoon we had a very fine view of the yet distant mountains, their white peaks standing out in bold relief against the blue sky. At 2, p.m., we resumed our march, the trail being none of the best, leading us sometimes down to the water edge, and again taking us to the high levels above, and sometimes through tangled bits of underbrush, where both hands were constantly needed to save the face from the branches and projecting bushes. At dusk we found ourselves nine hundred feet above the river, and had great difficulty in getting down to the lower terraces, along which we travelled in the dark, now and again missing the trail, and coming to a dead stop to look, or rather feel, for it, as the darkness was almost palpable. While going along slowly, our horses one and all took fright at a bear which we disturbed; but as we could not see him, he was left to his own devices. Our progress was now arrested by a large and strong mountain stream, beside which we encamped for the night.

Our first business the next morning was the construction of a raft, upon which, having embarked all our baggage and saddles, Kennedy, William and myself committed ourselves to the mercy of the Rivière du Milieu. The raft being made and tied together, we pushed off, each being furnished with a pole; but before we could well realize our position, the fragile and badly-constructed craft was hurled upon a large shoal, over which we bumped into the deep water below, losing at the same time several of the pieces composing the fundamental portion of our handiwork. By dint of the most desperate exertions and the utmost steadiness, we at length managed to reach an eddy, and then the shore, where we could afford to laugh at our own awkwardness. We certainly had a narrow escape! In the meantime the Indians, choosing a better place higher up, crossed in safety, having previously driven the horses into the water, and over to the other side.

By the appearance of the banks, both the Peace River and the Rivière du Milieu were low, although the latter must be very strong in early summer coming as it does from the eastern flanks of the mountains north of the Peace River. Its width was sixty yards, with an average depth of five feet: the water was much colder than that of the Peace. On riding up from the river to gain the higher regions above, we passed over some alluvial flats, which were very densely timbered, and we saw some magnificent rough bark poplars, three or four feet in diameter, and growing to a great height. We were now twenty-two miles from the lower end of the Rocky Mountain Portage, where we arrived on the morning of the 22nd, after following the northern slopes of the valley for the entire distance. Between the Rivière du Milieu and the Portage, we crossed several deep ravines, the outlets of small rivers flowing into the main one. The trail, though rough in occasional spots, carried us over a very fine country, where the excellent soil and large tracts of fine land, facing the south, would offer great facilities for farming. There was, however, a scarcity of wood, but the southern banks and the numerous islands, being covered with dense timber, afford unlimited quantities of that material for both fuel and manufacturing purposes. As we approached the foot of the Portage the soil became very light and sandy, and the cypress occurred in abundance. Sandstone rock began to show more frequently, and we now saw indications of a decided change in the formation of the country.

On reaching the level and sandy terrace immediately opposite "Hudson's Hope," the euphonious name of the Company's establishment, we could find no means of communication with the opposite shore;

but, after yelling ourselves hoarse, managed to draw the attention of a solitary miner, who was camped close to the Company's house. Carrying on a very trying conversation with this individual, the distance between us being about two hundred and fifty yards, and a high wind blowing, we found that Charlette, the man in charge, had gone down the river, and had taken with him the only canoe at the place, so that we had to give up all idea of crossing. There being yet no sign of the canoe with the botanist, we decided on proceeding over the Portage, after having rested our animals, and prepared our frugal mid-day meal. Hailing the miner again, he gave us the welcome news that there were several canoes at the head of the Portage, besides a large boat, the property of a prospecting party of miners, who had descended the Peace from the Omenica, and had left their boat there. From this point they had gone down to the Rivière du Milieu on a raft, and were there at this moment building canoes, with which to ascend that river. In fact, the party was within half-a-mile of ours on the morning which had nearly proved disastrous to us; but the high wind that then prevailed had effectually prevented our hearing one another. These miners, our friend informed us, were bound for the "Rivière aux Liards," where they expected to find gold in great and paying quantities. "Who are ye?" inquired our miner, "and where are ye goin'?" We replied,

"We are tourists, on our way to McLeod's Lake." "Well!" he answered, "ye'll have to hurry up; it's one hundred and sixty miles from here. Have you plenty grub?" We assured him on that score, and his answering yell was to the effect that we would likely get through all right, but it would be "touch and go" to take the boat so far at this late season.

Our dinner being despatched, we yelled a "good-bye" to our unapproachable informant, and faced the steep ascent up which the Portage trail led us. While ascending, we got an excellent view of the country south of Hudson's Hope. A level plateau immediately in rear of the Post was covered with a thick growth of poplars; but beyond, the rising ground was hidden by a dense spruce forest, in the midst of which nestled an outpost of the Company, situated on White Fish Lake, and which enjoys the unenviable notoriety of being greatly frequented by "grizzlies." The ferocious brutes are, doubtless, attracted thither by the fish, which they are adepts at catching whenever the shoaliness of the water admits, and they have on several occasions devoured some of the Company's horses.

Before leaving our dining camp, I was particularly careful to mark the indications of the aneroids, as upon the careful measurement of the difference in level between the head and foot of the Portage depended the correct estimate of the height of the river during its passage through the mountains, a problem I was very desirous to solve. On reaching the first high level, I found we were at an elevation of eight hundred feet above Hudson's Hope; but we continued to ascend, though very gradually, until abreast of the Portage Hill, when the highest part of the trail was reached. It was then half-past two o'clock, and our elevation was about eleven hundred feet above the water level at the lower end. The Portage road was passably fair, but the soil was sandy, supporting a growth of spruce trees and cypress. From this point our progress was downward, and we reached the level terraces, at the upper end, at half-past three in the afternoon, having been three hours and a-half in crossing. The road must be twelve or fourteen miles in length, as we lost no time, and trotted our horses occasionally. We were now fairly within the first range of the Rocky Mountains, which here are not to be compared, in point of elevation, with the mountains composing the same range at Jasper House. Several high and snow-clad peaks were, however, visible in the north-west.

About a mile below our camp, which we pitched close to a ruinous old log shanty, owned (as a ticket nailed to the door intimated) by "Bill Crust," a gentleman who combined the business of fur-trading with the occupation of a miner, the Peace River made the first step in the rapid succession of leaps which it takes during its course of twenty-five miles through the last barrier which the Rocky Mountains interpose between it and the Arctic Ocean. It here narrows to about one hundred and twenty yards, and, dashing impetuously between two not very high sandstone cliffs, disappears in the gloomy depths of the Canon.

Our first impulse, on arriving, was to look for the boat which belonged to the mining party; and, after a satisfactory examination, we proceeded to make preparations for the night; Mr. Kennedy proposing to return to the other end early the following morning, in order to meet Mr. Macoun and the rest of the baggage. At eight o'clock, Kennedy and I, having turned in, were about composing ourselves to sleep, when the wind, which had latterly been unsteady, veered to the south, and blew with such terrific violence that we were obliged to turn out and fell several large pines which stood in the vicinity, and threatened us with destruction. The cracking of falling trees was heard all night, and effectually banished sleep. The following evening, Mr. Macoun, Armstrong and the Indians, with the loaded horses, arrived. Charlette, the man in charge of Hudson's Hope, also made his appearance; and having now overhauled the boat, we determined to start the following forenoon. Having some doubts as to the capabilities of my Indian crew, I told Armstrong he might take passage with us; but he had elected to "paddle his own canoe;" so, giving him provisions for fifteen days, we left him to his own devices, and pushed off at one, p.m., on the 24th October. The boat being heavy, and the Indians perfectly unused to pulling an oar, we started with three men on the line, while William steered the unwieldy craft by the aid of a long sweep, and I took up a station in the bow with a pole. In this manner we made about six miles up stream, and camped upon the left bank. During the two following days we ascended the stream for a distance of thirty-six miles. The river was rather tortuous, and varied from a hundred and fifty to three hundred yards in width, and was sometimes split up into several channels, through which the current ran, with great velocity, over beds of gravel and boulders of limestone.

The mountains, during the first day's ascent, hardly deserved the name, for their elevation was not great; and on the left bank they were generally bare of timber, but covered with grass, through which numerous old buffalo and moose trails could be traced for miles. On the second day they increased in altitude; and on turning a bend in the river, we had a distant view of the high and snowy peaks of the main range, which now and again were obscured by heavy masses of snow clouds. A severe storm was evidently going on in those high and distant regions, and the ever-changing and fantastic shapes assumed by the storm-clouds were wonderful to behold, as they whirled around, and chased one another with marvellous rapidity. At one moment an immense and black mass of vapour would cover some towering peak, hiding it entirely from our sight, and the next instant would reveal the same mountain summit, in bold and glittering relief, bared to its very flanks, as if bidding defiance to the biting boreal blast.

Frequently long stretches of level terraces, the silt of bygone ages, occurred; but they generally ended abruptly at the base of some rocky and precipitous mountain flank, and sometimes shifted their position to the other side of the valley, where they met with similar obstructions.

On the morning of the 27th, having made about forty-two miles from "Bill Crust's" house at the head of the Portage, we reached a short rapid, called by the Hudson's Bay voyageurs, "*Le rapide qui ne parle pas*," owing to the fact of its being, in a high state of the water, almost smooth. Its fall could not have exceeded four feet; and though the current was very strong, we tracked up it in twenty minutes.

CHAPTER VI.

ROCKY MOUNTAIN PORTAGE TO STEWART'S LAKE.

Past the Rocky Mountains—The Parsnip—Hardihood of Indian Voyageurs—A Mining Pioneer—Lake McLeod—First Winter Camp—Sagacious Dogs—Route of the Canada Pacific Railroad—Lake Stewart—Salmon—Fort St. James—Hudson Bay Company and North-West Discontent.

IT had snowed during the previous night, and the round boulders being covered and slippery rendered tracking very laborious. We were now entering the highest range; but owing to the snow storms, which were holding a revel high up in the mountains, we lost the view of the gorgeous scenery which extended far above us. Now and again, only, did we catch a glimpse of some rugged peak towering four or five thousand feet above the eye. We camped about fourteen miles above the rapid; the current was strong all day, but the bed of the river was smooth, and had little fall. At five, p.m., on the 28th, we had cleared the Rocky Mountains, after passing some of the grandest and wildest scenery imaginable. During our passage through the highest

E

part of the range, the occurrence of level terraces was not so frequent as farther east, and in many places the steep and rocky mountain flanks abutted upon the water. Yet, with the advantages of an easily navigable river, the construction of a road through this valley would not be impossible, and at some future time *may* become an accomplished fact.

After passing Bernard's River, a little stream which empties its crystal waters into the Peace, just west of the highest range, we tracked on, having the advantage of a more uniform beach, and camped three miles above it, on the right bank. About five inches of snow covered the ground, and the underbush was loaded down with it, thus rendering camping very uncomfortable. The timber was very large in the vicinity of this camp, and had been so all through the heaviest part of the Rocky Mountain Valley. The next morning the botanist and I started on foot along the snow-covered beach for some distance; and after two hours' tracking we reached the foot of the "Finlay Rapids," which we surmounted by putting all hands, with the exception of the bowman and steersman, on the line. A projecting reef and a steep wall of rock occasioned some trouble, by causing William to keep the boat out to the extreme length of the line; and as those on shore were obliged to clamber over the rocky prominence, considerable risk was run. Having gained the upper end, without any accident to the boat, we tracked and poled up past the large island which divides the river immediately above the rapids. There was here a decided change in the colour of the water, that of the Parsnip, or south branch of the Peace River, being quite clear. After getting fairly into the south branch, we put ashore for dinner, which we prepared on rocks, exhibiting talc, slate and iron pyrites. No mountains were visible, excepting to north. Where we dined the banks were low, and covered with a thick growth of spruce, poplar and birch. The Parsnip was here a hundred yards wide, and the current very moderate in this short reach; but round the next bend we could see streaks of foam, an indication of swift water higher up. After dinner we tracked for five miles, when we camped among enormous poplars, four or five feet in diameter.

We had now really passed through the Rocky Mountains, in a large and unwieldy boat, manned by Indians, who had never handled an oar in their lives before. During our passage through this pass we had encountered only one slight rapid, the fall of which could not have exceeded five feet. With this trifling exception, the whole river, during the seventy miles which take it from the western side to the eastern wall of the range, falls very gradually, and the mean descent does not, I am sure, amount to twenty-four inches per mile of its course. The elevation of the Peace River being assumed to be fifteen hundred and ten feet at the head of the Portage, and sixteen hundred and fifty feet at the Finlay branch, the mean of those two elevations—fifteen hundred and eighty feet—may be taken as that of the Pass. It is needless to inform the reader that those elevations were not the results solely of barometric readings; but repeated observations of that instrument, combined with the inferential evidence derived from their relation to other known heights, confirm me in the belief that, at any rate, I am not *far* wrong.

Our ascent of the Parsnip continued for the next four days, during which time we had a decided preponderance of bad weather. The beaches were rarely free from snow, and ice could always be seen in spots shaded from the sun. We found the course of this stream extremely tortuous and rapid, while its bed was almost invariably of gravel—in many places, where we had occasion to cross and re-cross, being distinctly visible from one side to the other. Our progress was slow and laborious. Our four Indians, though dreadfully awkward in the use of the pole and oar, were quite indifferent to the ice-cold water, in which they often waded for hours up to their waists. William, the half-breed, though an active and powerful young fellow, could not equal them in that respect; and the nonchalance with which they took the water, while hauling on the line, excited his wonder and admiration, and, I may say, his jealousy also, for a half-breed hates to be outdone in matters which require those qualities so essential to a good Nor'-West traveller, viz., endurance of cold and hunger, and untiring strength.

I shall now content myself with giving an occasional extract from the diary of the voyage, and then take the reader to McLeod's Lake, which we reached on the 5th November.

"October 30th. — Under way at seven, a.m. Banks low; gravel bottom; poplars very large on banks; current two and a-half miles per hour; ice along the margin; cloudy; rising barometer. At dinner place, river one hundred and twenty yards wide. Water clear as crystal; very rough country on left hand; mountains well back from river.

"October 31st.—Under way at seven. Snow ceased; atmosphere cloudy. Plenty of beaver and otter along this river; their tracks very distinct and well beaten. Put ashore at half-past ten, a.m., to warm ourselves; boat coated with ice, and leaking badly. Gloomy weather; low banks all day, and have been so almost since we entered the Parsnip. Rocky Mountains range visible now and again on our left. At three, p.m., while tracking up a strong current, William, the steersman, was knocked overboard by the sweep, and nearly perished. Put ashore immediately, to build fire and camp."

Such were some of our daily jottings—laconic,

but suggestive of the situation. The thermometer during all this time ranged from 30 deg. to 33 deg., and we were thankful it was no colder. The scenery all along the Parsnip was extremely monotonous, and by the time we reached McLeod's River we were heartily sick of it. Twelve miles before arriving there, and on the 3rd November, while poling up along the banks, we were surprised to see a regularly organized white man's dwelling, and on hailing it, out stalked a solitary miner, Pete Toy by name, who shook hands very heartily with us all, and expressed no little astonishment at seeing us. Our first question was, "Whereabouts are we?" "Well," said he, "you are now about fourteen miles from the little river, and twenty-eight from the Fort, which you ought to reach to-morrow night." Pete was alone, but had a mate some six miles higher up. They were both engaged in trapping, and expected to make a good haul of beaver, marten and mink. They had abandoned their mining operations, which they could not follow up during the winter season, and intended trading with the few scattered Indians who usually frequented McLeod's Fort.

Pete was a fine specimen of the mining pioneer, tough as hickory, and clad in blue shirt, with his unmentionables tucked into his boots. His shanty was a pattern of neatness. This very intelligent man found perfect contentment in his lonely cabin, around which were hung the spoils of the chase, in the shape of beaver and marten skins, the latter much larger than those found east of the Rocky Mountains, and a huge skin which only the day before had roamed the trackless wild on the back of a grizzly. Mr. Toy gave us some delicious fresh bread, made from British Columbia flour. We, in return, presented him with a chunk of pemmican, manufactured at Fort St. John, of which we had an ample supply.

Declining his offer to make use of his cabin for the night, we pushed on, and camped a mile above, Pete promising to join us next day, as he, too, wished to go to the Fort. "Gentlemen," said Pete, as we were shoving off, "you may consider yourselves very lucky to have got through as well as you did; but I see you are prepared for the worst," pointing to the snow-shoes and other paraphernalia requisite for winter travelling, with which we had taken the precaution to furnish ourselves. "And mark my words," added he, "before three days, this 'ere river will be running ice; but you are all right now." The following evening we reached the little McLeod River, and were soon joined by Pete and Bill Southcombe, who overtook us in their "dug-out" of poplar.

We had now done with the Parsnip, and had navigated it for a distance of seventy-five miles. Its fall I estimate at eighteen inches per mile, and the construction of a road along its banks could be easily accomplished. But it is a very crooked stream, and the densely-wooded wilderness through which it flows is, owing to its rigorous climate, ill adapted for farming.

On the morning of the 5th we left our camp, and poled up the little river for seven miles, when we reached a lake, across which we pulled, and entered another small and shallow river, where we were obliged to abandon our boat, and transfer our baggage to a canoe, arriving at the outlet of McLeod's Lake at four, p.m., when we soon made ourselves at home in the Company's house. The next morning, with the assistance of Mr. Sinclair, the Company's agent, I paid off my four Beaver Indians, who had, indeed, behaved very well; and after settling up with William, another most excellent fellow, I started them all down to the boat, which they were to take back to the Rocky Mountain Portage. This they were unable to accomplish, being met by ice when half-way back; and I was told afterwards by Captain Butler, author of *The Great Lone Land*, that the poor fellows had to "foot it" for the rest of the distance, following the margin of the river, and having a wretched time of it as far as the Portage, which they reached in a very emaciated state. Messrs. Toy and Southcombe, after finishing their business, also took their departure; and the botanist and myself were left alone with Sinclair, who, with his Indian wife, were the sole residents of the place.

Lake McLeod.

It was a matter of much regret to me to find that there were no Indians about, as I had fully made up my mind to make a flying trip to the Summit Lake I have already alluded to, as being the source of one of the branches of the Pine River, as well as of another stream flowing down the western slopes of the Rocky Mountains to the south branch of the Peace; but having no guide, and the season being too late for an open trip, and too early for a winter one, I was reluctantly obliged to abandon the idea. On the night of the 6th, McLeod's Lake was partially frozen, and winter came on in right good earnest, there being already five or six inches of snow on the ground, although not sufficient to make snow-shoeing agreeable. After waiting several days in the expectation of meeting some Indians, I finally determined to start for Stewart's Lake (eighty-one miles distant), and, arranging with Sinclair to accompany us, we began to make the preparations necessary for the trip.

At seven, a.m., on the 9th, the thermometer marked 9 degrees; but the morning was beautifully clear, and at ten o'clock we turned our backs on Fort McLeod. Sinclair had provided a light sled, upon which our blankets and provisions were packed, and after harnessing four dogs to this vehicle, we set out on foot. Crossing the Long Lake River, we ascended a steep hill, and travelled steadily until three, p.m., when the roughness of the trail, and insufficient depth of snow, caused us to abandon the sled, and camp. The weather had now become very cold, the mercury standing at zero after sundown. This night we made our first winter camp of the season.

Having chosen a convenient spot, with plenty of green spruce and a sufficient quantity of dry wood at hand, one of us cleared away the snow, while another cut spruce branches, and the third chopped dry wood in lengths of eight or ten feet. Spreading the spruce on the ground to a depth of six inches or so, we arranged the wood in front, and soon had a roaring fire, by which we boiled water for tea, and were presently in the enjoyment of a good supper of pemmican, bread, and scalding hot bohea. After supper, we all devoted a half-hour to getting an extra supply of wood, which was piled up close at hand, to replenish the fire; and, spreading our blankets, we laid down with our feet to the blaze, and were soon snoring, with faces upturned to the clear and glittering sky. In a winter encampment, a covering is rarely if ever used, although sometimes a piece of thin sheeting cotton is spread behind, to break the force of the wind.

The following morning, at six o'clock, the mercury stood at ten degrees below zero, and the air was sufficiently keen to render the heat emitted by about a cord of blazing logs perfectly enjoyable. While breakfast was being prepared by one of us, the others gathered and packed our traps in bundles, adapted to the carrying capabilities of each individual. Neither were our canine friends forgotten, for Sinclair prepared four diminutive loads of about fifteen or twenty pounds each, with which we loaded each dog, which followed in our tracks with the gravity and decorum due to the occasion. It was amusing to watch the sagacious brutes when, by any chance, one or other of us lagged behind, as we sometimes did. One and all would then step aside, and courteously give the precedence, in order to benefit by the better beaten track. Sometimes one, more lazy than the rest, would calmly sit down and refuse to move, unmindful of the most seductive whistling and other blandishments; then a series of pantomimic gestures, accompanied by "bad" French, generally produced the desired effect.

The trail from McLeod's Lake to Long Lake, a distance of twenty miles, was very rough, owing to the windfalls and uneven nature of the ground. From that point to the Muskeg River, a stream flowing into the Fraser, the walking improved, but the soil throughout was useless. All this country is much cut up by lakes of great beauty, the waters of which abound in trout, and fish of various kinds. Furred animals are very numerous, especially martens; while deer, wolverine and bears are not by any means wanting.

Some seven or eight miles to the south-west of

McLeod's Lake, we passed over the highest point of land which is encountered between Lesser Slave Lake and Lake Stewart, a ridge lying between McLeod and Long Lake, the elevation of which was two thousand six hundred and sixty-five feet above the sea level. This was perfectly distinct from the *true watershed* separating the affluents of the Peace from those of the Fraser River, and which we crossed further on at the Muskeg River, elevated two thousand two hundred feet above the sea. The country immediately south-west of McLeod's Lake is very broken and hilly; but I believe that, should circumstances require the Canada Pacific Road to pass the Rocky Mountains, either by the Pine River Summit Lake Pass, or the Peace River Valley, the country between the Parsnip and Quesnel may be crossed, perhaps, under two thousand two hundred feet above the sea.

From the height of land we had a very fine view of the country away to the south-west; and Sinclair pointed out the position of Fort St. James, which bore north 125 degrees west, and was, probably, as the crow flies, forty miles distant. The general appearance of the landscape was tame, and the ground, cut up now and again by gullies, sloped gently towards Lake Stewart. The whole country was wooded, and the cypress, always indicative of wretched soil, predominated. Large burned tracts relieved the sameness of the aspect, and were easily recognized in the distance as white patches, where the snow had fallen, and now lay to a greater depth than in the green woods. A noticeable difference in the depth of the snow was observed as we crossed the watershed. North of it, its depth had been from six to eight inches, and had caused us much difficulty in walking; but now we had almost bare ground, which enabled us to push ahead with redoubled ease and speed.

At the Muskeg River we had engaged the services of a very intelligent Indian, to relieve us of a portion of our packs; so that now, with this additional help, and the better walking, our progress was much accelerated. Passing the upper part of the Salmon River, Dead Man's and Round Lake, we reached the edge of Carrier Lake, where we camped on the night of the 13th. The next morning we crossed Carrier Lake on the ice, which was perfectly glare, and fully nine inches thick; and making ten miles, we halted at Troisième Lac, where we prepared our dinner of partridges, shot that forenoon, fortunately for us, as our flour and pemmican were done. This, however, did not trouble us, being now within two and a-half hours of Stewart's Lake.

The soil began to improve a little during the course of this afternoon's walk, which took us occasionally through open pieces of level prairie. At four, p.m., we came in sight of the lake and Fort St. James, lying about three hundred feet below us.

Following the trail for a mile further, we reached the Hudson's Bay Company's establishment, where we were kindly welcomed by Mr. Gavin Hamilton, the agent. Here Mr. Macoun, my fellow-traveller, immediately prepared to leave for Victoria, and having procured for him a couple of Indian guides, to carry his bedding and provisions, we said good bye, and he took his departure for Quesnel on the 17th, reaching Victoria sometime in December, in perfect health, and the best of spirits, as I was afterwards glad to learn. My journey was, however, only half over, as I had instructions to proceed to Port Essington, on the Skeena. By Mr. Hamilton's advice I resolved to wait here until the ice on the lake was firmly set, and the season sufficiently advanced to admit of good snow-shoeing. I accordingly took up my quarters with Mr. Hamilton, who was extremely kind, and promised to procure the men I required to take with me to the Babine Post, which I intended to visit on my way to the Skeena. At this time, that portion only of Lake Stewart in the immediate neighbourhood of the Fort was frozen over, while the central and more northern parts were still open. This circumstance caused the postponement of my departure until the 2nd December, and afforded ample time for rest, together with the opportunity of carrying on meteorological observations, by which to obtain some clue to the actual elevation of this interesting locality above the sea.

Lake Stewart is a very beautiful sheet of water, about thirty-five miles in length, with an average width of five miles, and is, I should think, about eighteen hundred feet above sea-level. Its waters, together with those of Lakes Trembleur and Tacla, both very large lakes, find their way, by the Nakosla or Stewart's River, to the Fraser, which they join at Fort George. To the north and west the lake is flanked by high hills, and along some portions of the northern side precipitous rocks rear themselves high up from the very water's edge; but the southern extremity is bordered by very low and level land, which continues, I am told, to the Quesnel. The depth of this lake is generally very great, and salmon annually seek its waters, in which great quantities are caught by the Indians. This fish, in the dried state, forms the staple food of the natives, and is not only wholesome and palatable, but extremely nourishing, and is not looked upon with disdain by even the fastidious whites.

Fort St. James, the principal station of the Hudson Bay Company in the northern part of British Columbia, is nicely situated at the southern extremity of the lake, and commands a very fine view to the westward. Like all the interior posts of the Hudson Bay Company, it is composed of a few rough log houses, with a small potato patch and vegetable garden. The store or trading shop is usually supplied with excellent articles of clothing, blankets, cottons, and, in fact, all the stock necessary for the prosecution of the Indian trade, which is here, as at every other establishment of the Company, rapidly decreasing.

During the last fifteen years, this once powerful and deservedly successful institution has been on the decline; and dating from the death of its late energetic and far-seeing Governor, Sir George Simpson, the monopoly it was said to possess, and the influence attributed to its officers, existed only in the brains of its short-sighted and jealous opponents, who falsely gave it credit for a power and *prestige* utterly incompatible with recent events. We have only to look back upon the doings of Louis Riel, and the base ingrates who supported him in his nefarious acts, who forcibly, and under a false though specious pretext, wrested Fort Garry from the hands of those who had fed and clothed them for years—who turned, and, viper-like, stung the very bosoms from which they had drawn life and nourishment,—we have, I say, only to do this, and peer a little below the surface, to see how utterly unreasonable and groundless were the conclusions arrived at by those who, without a moment's consideration, pronounced a hasty and most partial verdict. In fact, for several years the Hudson's Bay Company, at Red River and on the Saskatchewan, has been the mere plaything of the half-breeds, who quickly took advantage of the false position in which the Company found itself soon after the withdrawal of the regular troops from Red River. In vain did the late Governor McTavish sue to the gentlemen living at their ease in London for help—in vain did he draw for them a true picture of the real state of affairs. They treated his suggestions with unmerited contempt, and pooh-poohed what they seemed to consider the fevered ravings of an over-worked brain. But William McTavish saw what others did not or would not see ; and the parsimonious policy of a few who would not even hear of a paltry company of fifty regulars, for the protection of life and property at Fort Garry, aided, no doubt, by the premature and uncalled-for interference of some Canadians, who thought they knew better than anybody else, precipitated the crisis which resulted in the lamentable events of 1869. No allusion is here meant to the one or two Canadian gentlemen then at Fort Garry on official business.

Other causes might be cited for the gradual decay of this yet great trading Company ; but this digression is foreign to the subject. It will, therefore, suffice to say that the introduction of liquors by petty traders, the infusion of new blood, which demands better wages and better food, and which has more extravagant notions than the simple yet hardy agents of the old school, who looked upon a chief factor much as a Persian water-seller regards the Shah, also the apathy with which some of the best officers in the service now regard the futile attempts to reorganize and ameliorate the present condition of affairs, are aids to the gnawing effects of the cankerworm, which is slowly but surely eating away the very vitals of this long established Company. But when this great corporation shall have wasted away, and when nothing but the mere fossil remains; when the "gem of the North West," the beautiful country of the Peace River, teems with a happy and thriving population, rich in the possession of countless flocks; when the Peace River coal and other products find a market in the east, and the Canada Pacific Railway shall issue excursion tickets to the Peace River Valley at ridiculously low prices, then Canada may remember that the long dead company was the pioneer of the North West, and chiefly instrumental in the bloodless conquest of British American Indians, to whose good-will and confidence the Company's honest policy has paved the way.

CHAPTER VII.

STEWART'S LAKE TO HAZELTON.

Comfortless Encampment—Trout Fishing Extraordinary—The City of Hog'em—Frying Pan Pass—Lake Babine—Paddling for Life—Little Babine and Susqua—Invited to Christmas.

BUT *revenons à nos moutons*, and I have here to crave the indulgence of the generous reader, who has borne me company so long, and who, perhaps, may have the curiosity to know how I fared on my solitary trip through the trackless wastes of Northern British Columbia. Well, after seeing the "lions" of Fort St. James, and enjoying the hospitality of Mr. Gavin Hamilton; after dining in great comfort with poor Judge Fitzgerald (since gone to his account), and his deputy, Captain Fitzstubbs, a fine, handsome, jovial fellow, in whose company—must I confess it?—some of the saloon keeper's brandy (for Stewart's Lake had reached that pitch of civilization, and actually could boast of a regularly organized whisky shop, where brandy-smashes, cocktails, and three card "monte" helped to ease the reckless miner of his hard-earned gains), found its way, in a temperate kind of style, down our throats, I very reluctantly resumed my weary tramp, which was to cease at whatever point on the coast I might be lucky enough to find the Hudson Bay Company's steamer, the *Otter*. Having secured the services of a Red River half-breed named Damare, and three others, all Indians, or "fractional parts" of that persuasion; having put up a good supply of bacon, beans, flour, tea and sugar, and being each provided with snow-shoes, mocassins, and plenty of blankets, I said farewell to Fort St. James, and took my departure for Fort Babine on foot. It was noon when we left: the ice being quite glare, and the men willing, we made ten miles in about a couple of hours, and camped on the west side of the lake. On reaching that shore we found, to our annoyance, that the ice was extremely thin, and, a little further on, there was open water. Our camp was made on a sloping rock within half-a-dozen feet of the water edge, for we could find no better ground. Dry wood was scarce, and after a fire was lighted we were nearly smoked to death, the wind having risen, causing us great inconvenience and discomfort. We were now without a tent, but carried with us a piece of factory cotton, which we stuck up behind us on poles, but speedily hauled down again, finding it do more harm than good. During the night snow began to fall, and this melting on our blankets from the heat of the fire, rendered matters more uncomfortable still. This was truly a most wretched encampment, and was only the beginning of a series. While reclining on our angular bed, we could still see the distant lights of the fort, and I most heartily wished myself back again in its snug quarters. The night was moderately warm, and we woke up next morning glad to relieve our aching bones, and anxious to get rid of our stiffness by good exercise, of which we soon got plenty, as we had no longer any ice to walk on, and were obliged to follow the rugged beach, sometimes coming to a projecting rocky point, the steep sides of which we had to clamber. Sometimes, indeed, we had to take to the woods for short distances, and altogether we had a rough time of it.

The lake was now entirely open, and by 4, p.m., we had only reached a point opposite the Indian village of Pinche. We camped here, and, wearied by the exertions of the day, soon fell asleep.

Dec. 4th.—Tried the ice again this morning, but found it very weak ; progress slow, being obliged to proceed cautiously, sounding the ice with poles as we went along. No getting to the Portage this day. N.W. and S.E. is the general direction of the lake. During the afternoon had good and sound ice for the rest of the day, and camped opposite Tache Village. Ice nine inches thick, but an Indian from the village tells us that a few miles above the lake is open to the very end, so more trouble looms up for to-morrow.

December 5th.—Travelled eight miles on the ice, and were again met by open water; halted for dinner, and sent on two of the young lads to the Portage for a canoe.

We left the baggage here, and the rest of us proceeded along the margin when practicable. After two hours of execrable walking, during which slips and falls were the rule, and upright walking was the exception, we reached the solid ice at the upper end; a short walk took us to the little river, on the banks of which we camped.

I now determined to send on two men to the Babine Lake, seven or eight miles distant, with the heaviest of my baggage. They were then to start for Fort Babine by canoe, this lake usually remaining open till the end of January, while Damare, another man, and myself, were to branch off to the right, towards Lac Trembleur, whence I intended to strike north towards Lake Tacla, and then make for Fort Babine by "Leon's trail."

Having reached the first little lake in the middle of the portage, our party split up, two men proceeding to the Babine end of the portage, myself and two others following up this little lake for three or four miles, when we left it and immediately took the ice on another. Following this one for a mile or two, we came upon a large camp of Indians who were catching the finest trout and white fish I ever saw. They had thousands of them hung up on poles to dry. Their encampment was a perfect picture, what with the primitive and open lodges, the long rows of fish in the successive stages of desiccation, the half naked children sprawling about in the snow, the dogs too fat and lazy to move, and the numerous dug-outs or canoes hauled up on the beach. This lake was encircled by high hills, and the portion of it which we had come over, was hard and fast for the winter; while just here it was perfectly open and free from ice. We camped here for the purpose of getting one of those Indians to guide us to "Gus Wright's trail," which I was desirous of reaching by a short-cut over the mountains.

The next morning we started in a canoe for the upper end of the lake, and resuming our snow-shoes, ascended the steep and rugged hills lying south-west of Lake Trembleur, keeping due north all the while. This was a very rough and disagreeable piece of road, and we were not sorry to get on to the so-called steamboat trail. It must be remarked here that a stern-wheel steamer was laid up for the winter in Lake Trembleur. This vessel, which I did not see, had been brought up the Fraser, the Nakosla River, through Stewart's Lake, and by the connecting stream, to its present winter quarters. It was owned, I believe, by one Gus Wright, who purposed to start a freight business between Lake Trembleur and the

Tacla Landing, whence it is only a matter of about fifty miles to the " City of Hog'em," the capital, if I may apply such a term, of the Peace River gold mining regions. There are several ways by which these as yet embryo diggings may be reached from Victoria. The intending miner may, if he chooses, take steamer to Port Essington, six hundred miles up the coast, and thence ascend the Skeena to the infant town of Hazelton, otherwise more generally known as " The Forks." This implies the ascent (and a very difficult one it is) of this rapid, and, as it has proved to not a few unfortunates, fatal stream, for a distance of about one hundred and fifty miles. Leaving the treacherous waters of the Skeena, he may then proceed either on foot or on horseback to the Babine Lake, some fifty or sixty miles distant, crossing the lower extremity of which he keeps on by the same means to Tacla Landing, thirty or forty miles further, during which time he must cross a high mountain range by a pass known as that of the " Frying Pan." From the landing the mines are easily reached by a pretty fair trail.

The Fraser River presents another route. One may take stage to Quesnel, thence proceed on foot or on horseback across a partly level country to Fort St. James, whence a passable trail takes one to the Nation River ferry, from which there is a trail to Germansen Creek, and the Omenica ; or instead of leaving the Fraser at Quesnel, the tourist may still follow that river until he reaches the Giscombe Portage. This must then be crossed, and launching his canoe in the waters of Summit Lake, the traveller may descend, aided by a very gentle current, the waters flowing into McLeod, whence eighty-nine miles of good and rapid navigation will take him to the Finlay branch. Here he must ascend the rapid current of the Omenica, for seventy-five miles, when Germansen Creek will be reached, and if he chooses to visit the capital, fifty miles more of the same tortuous stream will bring him within sight of the spires (?) of "Hog'em." But all these routes are difficult, involving long and fatiguing journeys on foot, and navigation of a dangerous nature, which the miner is too often ready to try in craft ill-suited to the occasion. Hence the numerous and painful accidents which, like those of the fall of 1871, shock the less adventurous residents of Victoria. But I am again digressing.

We reached the steamboat trail which there skirted the shores of a rather large and beautiful lake, on the other side of which a high and conspicuous snow capped mountain, very clearly visible from Fort St. James, reared its glittering white summit high in the cold morning air. Our course was now about west, and Gus Wright had certainly picked out a very fair road, the country through which it lay being passably level; but the walking was heavy, as there was too little snow for snow-shoeing, and deep drifts which we occasionally came across rendered it heavy work.

We reached Lake Babine after having followed Gus Wright's trail for a distance of twenty miles, and found the bay upon which we debouched hard and fast: open water, however, lay about a mile out. While crossing on the ice to the open, we scanned the shore anxiously for a canoe, and after a long search discovered a leaky and worn out "dug-out," hauled up on a rocky point. On reaching it, we found that it was very badly injured, so set to work repairing it, and making paddles, of which there were none to be seen. Four of those indispensible adjuncts were roughly and rapidly hewn out of a spruce tree, and transferring our baggage and provisions to this wretched apology for a canoe, we embarked, but found the craft so unsteady, that great care was necessary to prevent our upsetting.

To make matters worse, the canoe leaked like a basket, and we were obliged to put ashore upon an island to patch her up in the best way we could. After some delay, we started again, intending to paddle all night in order to reach Fort Babine without camping; but we were destined to have a taste of what this immense and deep body of water could do when roused to anger by a stiff Sou' Wester. The afternoon had been unusually dark and gloomy, and as the short day drew to a close, the deep waters of the lake assumed a sombre tint, which, deepened by the dark and angry-looking sky, was excessively depressing to the spirits. As daylight disappeared, the wind, which until now had been very light, began to rise in sudden gusts, causing a long and heavy swell, which now and again, as if indignant at our audacity, struck our frail craft, and drenched us to the skin with its cold spray. The now rapidly increasing gale was happily in our favour, and giving up all hope of going on that night, we determined to beach our canoe at the very first opportunity. We accordingly steered for a deep sandy bay which lay a full mile to leeward. But in order to reach it, we had to weather a rocky point, which projected far into the seething lake, and upon which, if we had failed to clear it, our miserable craft would have inevitably been dashed into pieces. The chattering tongues of my Indian crew were now stilled, and the paddles struck the water with redoubled force, for we all felt that the safety of our property, nay our very lives, perhaps, depended upon getting past the rocky shore, which loomed up on our right, cold, dark, and the very picture of desolation. Beyond the reach of the waves and spray, snow to the depth of nearly a foot covered the surface, and helped to light up the gloomy picture. A few strokes of the paddle, and we had cleared the danger, and now headed for the low shingly beach, where we ran the canoe high up in the snow and immediately emptying her of the contents, turned her up beyond the reach of the waves.

The night was now far advanced, and as we could not pace the beach until daylight, we with great reluctance set about camping, an operation which, in the darkness, proved not only tedious but difficult. The men were wearied, too, and hungry, and for the first time lost their equanimity of temper. The work, in consequence, proceeded slowly, and in sullen silence. To add to our difficulties, dry wood and brush to lie or sit on were very scarce, and another day had begun ere a passable fire and some hot tea had restored us all to our usual frame of mind. We then composed ourselves to sleep, and woke as the first grey streaks of dawn appeared on the morning of the 11th.

My first care on awaking was to strike a match under the blankets, and steal a glance at my watch and barometer. The first indicated the hour of six, and the second 27·19 inches—a rather low reading. On sitting up and looking around, the prospect was anything but cheering; during our sleep five inches of snow had fallen, our fire was completely out, and the forms of my three men, curled up under their blankets, were just visible as they lay buried beneath a warm covering of snow. The wind still kept up, while the yet angry waves beat upon the beach with a mournful cadence, which seemed to exert a somnolent influence upon the quiet forms beside me. A "hallo!" repeated many times, at last induced them to rise from their slumber, and, one by one, after lazily shaking off the snow, they proceeded to start a fire. Under its influence, and fortified by a breakfast of smoking hot tea, flanked by a frying pan piled up with a pyramid of baked beans, from which peeped sundry luscious pieces of Oregon bacon, our energies returned, and we hastily launched and loaded our canoe, and pushed off for Fort Babine, yet distant about fifteen miles. Lake Babine is an immense body of water, probably eighty or ninety miles long, with a breadth varying from four to ten miles. It is extremely deep, has numerous islands, and is bounded, on nearly every hand, by high, rocky and densely wooded shores. That portion of it which I saw struck me as bearing a wonderful resemblance to Lake Temiscamingue on the Upper Ottawa.

At noon the wind had entirely chased away the dark vapoury clouds which, during the last few days, had obscured the heavens, and by three o'clock, when we stepped ashore at the Company's Fort, a hard frost had set in, which promised to speedily bind down the deep waters of the lake with the icy grasp of winter. A group of wondering Indians were at the beach to receive us, and a general hand-shaking had to be gone through before I could venture to enter the cosy house of St. Pierre, the man in charge, who then happened to be absent at the fishery situated near the lower end of the lake. As there was no one to dispense the few necessary articles needed for the rest of my journey to the Forks of Skeena,

I assumed the double duties of seller and buyer by taking possession of the Company's store, and commenced weighing out sundry lots of flour, tea and sugar, not forgetting the "institution" of British Columbia—bacon and beans. Having duly entered those items with scrupulous care in the Company's blotter, I prepared for another stage, by sending off Damare and another man to the Fishery, by the ice, while I, with two newly hired Indians, got together supplies for the next stage of the journey. My new travelling companions were odd looking specimens in their way. One was an elderly individual of about fifty who possessed but one eye, the vacant socket being covered with a green patch which was far from improving its owner's hang-dog look. His mate was recommended to me by Damare, as a most valuable man, being a perfect master of the French language. So his patron said. I found afterwards that his knowledge of French was limited; his sole vocabulary consisting of the adverbs *oui* and *non*, which he used on every possible occasion, regardless of consequences. Both he and "One-eye," however, belied their looks very much, proving to be active and willing, the man with the patch especially maintaining a uniform and agreeable temper throughout.

With the exception of the Post at McLeod's Lake, I think Fort Babine is one of the most wretched holes I ever saw. It is situated on the north-east side of the lake of the same name, and is within twenty-five miles of its northern extremity and outlet. West of the Fort the lake is very narrow, but again widens out northwards, and from this strait it was completely frozen over to the Indian village, whither Damare had gone. Right opposite, to the eastward, and about two miles across the bay, a trail takes up through a slight gap in the high hills towards the outlet of Lake Tacla and the Nation Lakes. This is another way to the Omenica, but is seldom used by miners. A few miles behind, to the north east of the Fort, a high mountain forms a conspicuous landmark. The establishment consists of three or four log houses, and is of little importance to the Company. On the 13th December I left the Fort accompanied by "One-eye" and the "Linguist." We had the advantage of a beautiful day, and walked at a good pace over the ice and along St. John's Bay, towards its upper end, where, seven or eight miles from the Fort, the waters of another system of lakes join those of the Babine.

Following a pretty little stream for a couple of miles we again travelled the ice on a narrow sheet of water, eleven miles in length, and parallel to Lake Babine. Two other good sized lakes belonging to the same chain were then followed, when we took to the left and made for the Babine lake again. During this short stage the snow had only been nine inches in depth, but the temperature was low, the thermometer having generally stood at from 20 deg.

to 25 deg. below zero. It was a fine bright Sunday morning when my two men and I descended to the Indian village known as "The Fishery." We straightway made for the Company's store, then unoccupied, a miserable, unfinished log shanty, through the interstices and chinks of which the cold, biting frost penetrated, and chilled us to the bone. Damare, however, who had arrived the day before, had already made the place as comfortable as possible, and a big fire blazed in the open chimney, while on the hearth sundry pots and pans contained material for a meal, to which we all three did justice. This fishery is quite close to the outlet of the lake, the waters of which, after following the circuitous and extremely rapid River Babine for a distance of sixty or seventy miles, empty into the Skeena above Fort Stager, the point to which the American Western Union Telegraph Company brought the line which was to have connected North America with Asia.

We remained in this place until the following morning, when we parted company; Damare and his comrade returning to Babine Fort, while I and my two Babine Indians, together with a third man, crossed the lake (here not over two hundred yards wide), and commenced the ascent of a mountain range, lying nearly north and south, separating the Babine system from the waters of the Wotsonqua, a southern tributary of the Skeena. For seven or eight miles we ascended through a thick forest of spruce and balsam, some of the latter of great size, and finally reached the summit of the pass, when the aneroids marked 25 in. with a temperature of 5 deg. above zero. Three and a half hours before, while yet on the ice of Babine lake, the same instruments stood at 27.47 in., and thermometer at 16 deg. below zero. This was by far the greatest altitude I had yet attained, and from this elevated locality a most magnificent *coup d'œil* of the Susqua valley was obtained. Immediately to the right, and distant probably two or three miles, a high and snow-capped peak towered far above, while before me, deep down in the valley, the Susqua followed its westward course for fully thirty miles, until deflected to the north by the huge mountain mass of the Rocher Deboule range, which formed a bold and picturesque background. High mountains to the north and south hemmed in the valley of this now tiny stream, which, for the first few miles of its course, flowed quietly enough over a very gradual incline, but afterwards gathering fresh impetus, dashed on through a series of rocky canons, to join its sister stream, the Wotsonqua. At this great elevation, probably four thousand feet above the sea, the snow was only three feet in depth, and some stunted cypresses were the only trees to be seen. The ground began to dip immediately after crossing the summit, and following the trail for a few miles, we descended to the bottom of a deep ravine, through which flowed a small rivulet. The steep sides of this rocky gully not offering level ground sufficient for our camp, we made it upon the ice, after laying down a plentiful supply of green spruce branches. The little creek which could be distinctly heard as it trickled beneath us over its rocky bed, supplied us with good water for our tea, thus sparing us the tedious operation of producing that *sine qua non* from melted snow. A capital fire being built upon the edge of the bank, our camp soon assumed its usually comfortable appearance, despite its icy floor, which, had it given way, would have produced consequences both disagreeable and serious.

After breakfast the following morning, I strolled down the creek to examine the source of the little Babine and Susqua rivers, which lay eight hundred feet below the summit level. Twenty minutes walking on snow-shoes brought me to the narrow strip of swamp out of which issue the two streams; the one making a leap eastward, of sixteen hundred feet in a distance of nine miles, into Lake Babine; the other seeking the Wotsonqua, which lies fully thirty miles to the westward, and about 2,400 feet below the level of this one's source. The steep and towering mountain mass which bounded the southern side of the valley cast a deep gloom on every side, and the silence of this dark ravine was positively awful. Taking a hurried survey of the place, I retraced my steps, and was right glad to regain the now deserted camp fire, the Indians having started during my absence. Six miles further we took the ice on the Susqua, and followed it for a few miles. The water had fallen, consequently the ice was unsupported, and we broke through several times. The descent of this mountain stream was very great, in some places the aneroids indicating a fall of two hundred and fifty feet to the mile. While walking along, one of the Indians fell through and was severely hurt, so we were obliged to camp, having made a very poor day's journey.

On the 18th we left camp, fully determined to reach " The Forks " that night. The weather had now changed, and a slight fall of snow set in, totally obscuring the bold mountain scenery. On getting down a couple of thousand feet below the summit we found the ground almost bare, and had capital walking for some distance. At three in the afternoon the road again became rough, numerous deep ravines intersecting our path, necessitating painful and laborious ascents and descents. Some of those gullies were three hundred feet in depth, and great care was required in wending up and down their steep and icy sides. We often had to haul ourselves up by the branches, but the men stuck to it bravely, and by four o'clock we were within fifteen miles of Hazelton. Although night was just coming on, we made a fire by which to boil our tea-kettle, and at five o'clock renewed our journey in Indian file, my French speaking Indian taking the lead. At every resting place I enquired into our dead reckoning, but my questions usually eliciting the most ridiculous answers from the Indians, I remained in complete ignorance as to our whereabouts until we reached the very edge of the plateau immediately in rear of the village. Midnight had just gone, when, through the now thickly falling snow, the Indian pointed to the scattered collection of log huts one hundred and fifty feet below, which was dignified by the name of Hazelton.

In front of this silent village the Skeena could be distinguished by the black line of its unfrozen waters, down which coursed—tumbling, tossing, and grinding against each other, as if eager for precedence—huge, white floes of ice. With the exception of this narrow streak of rapid water, the entire landscape was white, and desolate to a degree. On our left, deep down in the hollow, we could see several Indian huts of wretched construction, partially lighted up by the fitful glare of their watch fires, while the dismal chants and "rattling" of the medicine men were heard, as they performed their heathenish rites over the departing spirit of some relative, laid low by the ravages of an epidemic then rife amongst them. A steep sideling trail had been cut down the bank, and we were just preparing to descend, when I, incautiously approaching too near the brink, slipped upon the icy ground, and reached the lower level before my companions, who, immensely amused at the exploit, followed in a more leisurely manner. We at once sought out Tom Hankins' store, where, after a little delay, Tom himself appeared, and gave me a hearty welcome. "Just in time for Christmas," said Tom; and instantly called up "Charlie," the cook—a fat, good natured Indian of the Hyder tribe—who poked up the fire, and with the celerity of a city waiter, soon placed before me hot tea and eatables. "Just in time for Christmas week. We're going to have a time of it, and you may make up your mind to remain here for three weeks, until there is good going. It's no use," said he, as I deprecated such a long delay; "not an Indian will budge from here until the New Year, anyhow, so you may keep cool." To confess the truth I did not feel averse to spending a few days with such a hospitable entertainer, and, convinced of the soundness of his argument, I resigned myself to the delay consequent upon a fortnight's sojourn at "The Forks." After partaking of a homeopathic dose of hot-scotch, we separated for the night, Charlie, the cook, having provided me with a "shake-down" on the floor, where I speedily forgot all my troubles, and slept very soundly till seven, a.m., when I was awakened by the preparations for breakfast. As we sat down to that meal, Tom introduced his wife, a very nice, agreeable person, who seconded her husband's endeavours towards my comfort.

CHAPTER VIII.

HAZELTON.

Physical Features—The Skeena—An Indian Ranche—Romantic Bridge—Curious Carving—Christmas at the Diggings—Up the Skeena—The Wotsonqua—A "Cholera Box"—American Enterprise at fault—A hideous Canon—Characteristics of Miners.

HAZELTON, or "The Forks," as it is generally designated, owes its origin to the Hudson's Bay Company, which formerly, and until within a few years back, had a fur-trading post a mile or so lower down than the site of the present little town. About a score of log houses composed the village, which is situated between the forks of the Skeena, and its tributary the Wotsonqua. The surrounding country is essentially mountainous, and the scenery magnificent. Five or six miles to the southeast, a high range of mountains, the same alluded to already as that of the Rocher Deboule, stands out in bold relief, and from its great height (probably five thousand feet or thereabouts,) appears almost to hang over the little town. To the westward, and on the opposite side of the Skeena, another very high mountain, its summit probably ten miles distant, and bare of vegetation, bounds the view in that direction, and heightens the picturesque aspect of the scenery. All around are dense forests of spruce, poplar and other woods, while the low valleys are, with the exception of some level terraces along the river banks, rough and much broken up. The Skeena at this village is probably one hundred and fifty yards wide, and was rapidly closing up. The distance from Hazelton to Port Essington, at the mouth of the river on the Pacific coast, is estimated to be one hundred and fifty miles, and during the greater part of its course toward the sea, it is obstructed by numerous rapids, the navigation of which is difficult, and often dangerous. A mile below Hazelton the Wotsonqua, a south-eastern tributary, enters the Skeena. This river takes its rise some eighty miles from its mouth, to the west of Lake Babine; and for the greater part of that distance flows through a succession of deep rocky canons. The Susqua enters the latter some eighteen miles from Hazelton.

Several bands of Indians live and hunt in the vicinity of the Forks. They are generally of a peaceable disposition, and work for the whites with alacrity and good-will. About three miles from Hazelton, and three hundred feet down in the rocky bed of the Wotsonqua, there is a large Indian ranche, or village, of some twenty houses, called the "Achwylget." Immediately in front of it the Indians have thrown a suspension bridge across the rocky chasm, through which the waters of the Wotsonqua rush with impetuous haste towards the Skeena. Here the scenery is wild, and sufficiently picturesque to please the most ardent lover of nature. The bridge is built entirely of wood, fastened together by withes and branches; its height above the roaring waters beneath is fifty feet, and it sways about under the weight of a man, to try even the nerves of a Blondin.

Several very elaborately carved and lofty crest poles stand in front of the principal houses of this ranche. Those are generally hewn out of large pines, often sixty feet in height, and from base to top are carved many curious figures, representing bears, toads, fish and creatures of mythical origin. Some of the carving is so well done as to equal the best work I have ever seen executed by the New Zealanders, who excel in that art. The carvers of those poles often spend many months in their construction, and the amount of ingenuity displayed and labour expended varies directly as the rank and wealth of the chief whose motto or crest they are intended to represent. At the butt, some uncouth and hideous animal, a puzzle to the most expert palæontologist, is cut out of the wood, and as the spar tapers upwards, the figures diminish in size, and become of less elaborate design, until, upon the very pinnacle the ridiculous and grotesquely carved figure of an aboriginal, pipe in mouth, and capped by a plug hat, entirely destroys the effect of what is, otherwise, very often, a really fine work of art.

The houses are of great size, but with few pretensions to comfort, and always have a large fire-place in the middle, round which from fifty to one hundred persons can find accommodation. The doors of some of those dwellings were well worthy of inspection. One house in particular was entered through the folding jaws of some nondescript animal, which, as you entered, snapped and shut down upon you with a semblance of savage ferocity, almost akin to reality. Those large ranches are generally deserted during the winter months, when the Indians retire to the shelter of the woods, where fuel is more easily obtained, and the trapping of different furred animals can be prosecuted with advantage. A little below Hazelton there is another Indian village, but of small extent, and, like that of the Achwylget, it was also abandoned by its usual denizens. Those were the first really large and well-built dwellings of Indians I had yet met with, but, as the reader will see, if he follows me to the coast, they were insignificant when compared with the immense and comfortable houses of the tribes living in more immediate proximity to the sea.

My first visit after breakfasting with Tom, was to his partner, Mr. McK——, who lived in an adjoining house. These gentlemen were engaged in the fur trade, and carried on, besides, a miscellaneous traffic with passing miners, of whom there were some score or more then wintering at the "Forks." As might have been expected, there was, besides the dwelling-houses and stores, a saloon, which formed the favourite resort of the residents during their hours of leisure, when " poker," " euchre " " and forty-five " absorbed the attention of the jovial and reckless population. Owing to the want of accommodation at Hankins' house, I shifted my quarters to the saloon, and was located in a log-house, containing but one room and a closet, where the bar-tender kindly provided me with a bedstead, on which I hoped to pass, after a civilized fashion, a few really comfortable nights ; but unfortunately for me, I reckoned without my host, and did not calculate upon the disorganization consequent upon the rioting and festivities of Christmas week, then close at hand. The weather had again become settled, and on the morning of Christmas eve the thermometer stood at twenty-two degrees below zero. This was, however, a much higher temperature than is usually experienced at this place. I was informed that the previous winter forty, and even fifty, degrees below zero had been, by no means, exceptional readings at the corresponding period.

From early morning until far into the evening the miners and every one else at the place were busily occupied in getting up shooting matches and other games, with which to usher in the time-honoured holiday ; and at midnight of the 24th, the bursting of a bomb consisting of 25 pounds of gunpowder securely tied up in many thicknesses of strong canvas, announced the day which Englishmen so much delight to respect. Simultaneously a dropping fire of muskets and revolvers, accompanied by shouts and yells from the excited crowd, resounded through the air, and forthwith the major part of the population of Hazelton crowded into the saloon, where ample justice was done to the occasion in many a flowing bumper, the exciting effects of which were soon manifested by eager demands for music and dancing. An old accordeon and tambourine, the only instruments at the place, were called into requisition, while the crack dancers took the floor, among whom, and chief of them all, figured Dancing Bill, of British Columbian renown. The fun grew fast and furious ; the legitimate instruments already in use, and soon rendered almost unserviceable, were not found sufficient to satisfy the terpsichorean tastes of the miners ; frying pans, pokers, shovels, anything, in fact, capable of producing sound, were therefore added to the list, and helped to swell the din become now almost demoniacal. To sleep through such an uproar was, of course, out of the question ; so, seizing the first opportunity, I made myself scarce, and sought refuge in a neighbouring shanty, where I managed to elude the vigilance of the noisy crowd, and snatch several hours of quiet rest. These demonstrations of mirth and loyalty continued for several days, and, to avoid them, I was glad of the occasion to make a short tour of exploration around the base of the Rocher Deboule and up the Wotsonqua, in which I was joined by Tom, who had now become sick and tired of the several days' consecutive festivity.

After a short journey up the Skeena in the direction of Kyspyox, with McK—— for my companion, when we photographed several places of interest—amongst others, Hazelton and the mountains in its vicinity—Tom Hankin and I, accompanied by Charlie and another Indian, started on a little tour up the Wotsonqua, taking with us my camera, which Tom, facetiously, and as it turned out, unfortunately, chose to designate by the rather inappropriate name of the "Cholera Box." In order to explain, it is necessary to remark that a few months previous Mr. T., the gentleman in charge of the Mission Station at the mouth of the Naas River, had paid a pastoral visit to the Achwylget Indians. With his other *impedimenta* he had brought a small magic lantern and slides, which were duly exhibited to their wondering gaze, not without a certain amount of pomp and ceremony. After the reverend gentleman's departure, however, it most unfortunately happened that a species of cholera broke out among the native Hazeltonians; the origin of which they most illogically attributed to the "one-eyed devil" in the lantern and its exhibitor. Once possessed of the idea, which the native medicine men did their utmost to encourage, the reasoning and arguments of the whites were unavailing; and as the disease spread, so did the belief in the occult powers of Mr. T—— gain ground. This was Tom's story, and he added that perhaps it was just as well for Mr. T—— that he had " mizzled" before serious consequences ensued. With this unfortunate precedent the reader may imagine that I was not unnaturally a little shy of parading the camera, an instrument bearing a certain family likeness to the hated lantern, and which my friend Tom would persist in calling by such an obnoxious name. As luck would have it, after we were out a couple of days, the Indian, who made the photographic apparatus his particular burthen, was taken suddenly ill one evening in camp. We had noticed certain peculiarities in his behaviour, and had, on several occasions, observed him eyeing the dreaded box with looks of evident aversion. When turning in on that particular evening, Tom remarked in his sententious way : " I'll bet the treats that fellow's berth will be vacant to-morrow morning." And when we got up the following day, we found his prophetic speech verified, for no Indian was to be seen but Charlie, who said the fellow had gone off, evidently in mortal terror of the box and its mysterious contents. Tom and I thus fell in for equal shares of the remaining load, while Charlie, being a Hyder, and above such superstitious fears, shouldered the box without comment.

Upon several occasions during this little tour, we came upon the remains of the Western Union Telegraph Company's line, and at one particular stage of our trip, followed for several miles the wide and well cut-out trail which had been opened for that purpose. The reader may possibly not be aware of the fact that, several years ago, the Western Union constructed a telegraph line from Quesnel to Kyspyox, intending to carry it northwards to Behring's straits, where, by a cable, it was to have connected with the Asiatic shores, and, after being carried over the vast Siberian Steppes, with Europe. This was previous to the successful termination of the North Atlantic Company's operations, which, of course, put a stop to further attempts in this direction. The wide and thoroughly cut-out trail still remains, but the poles have been ruthlessly cut down by the Indians, who stole the insulators, and made use of the wire for various purposes. Tons of that expensive material still lie in the dreary depths of the British Columbian forests, while immense coils are yet in store at the now deserted post, Fort Stager, the relics of a vast undertaking, and a silent tribute to American enterprise.

Before returning to the Forks, we followed the lofty banks of the Wotsonqua, and made several ineffectual attempts to cross it. For miles this stream flows at the bottom of a hideous canon, which we found impossible to descend. The scenery was of the very wildest, and, but for the constant fall of snow, would have furnished some fine photographs. As it was, we were obliged to content ourselves with a hurried examination, obtained often at great risk, for the perpendicular and rocky walls of this Styx-like river were of immense height, and the steadiest nerves were required to enable one to reach a position from whence the dreary depths of the abyss could be seen. On our return we found all hands in a state of convalescence, and quietly settling down again to their usual humdrum life.

During conversations I had on different occasions with the miners then wintering at Hazelton, I gathered that the operations of the last season had not been very successful. A few, as usual, had made fair wages, but the majority had only spent their time and labour in the chimerical pursuit of wealth, and had returned, some to Victoria, and a few to this place, poorer in purse and health than at the commencement of the season, but still brimful of hope and perfectly sanguine as regarding the next spring's work. The miner is truly a wonderful combination of pluck and endurance; although often unfortunate, he is never discouraged. After years of unrequited labour, he generally returns to the scenes of former operations with renewed hope, or shouldering his blankets he roams, very often alone, over rugged mountains, through dense forests, across rapid and dangerous rivers, in pursuit of that gold which too often proves a curse to its possessor. He is generous to a degree, and will share his last crust and spend his " bottom " dollar in treating a friend. In his cups, he is sometimes an ugly customer, but in that respect he is no worse than his neighbours. In nine cases out of ten, he is a lover of law and order, at any rate, such was the character given of those operating upon the Omenica by Judge Fitzgerald, who, during his tenure of office at those diggings, and aided by one constable only, rarely, if ever, had trouble in adjusting the difficulties arising in those remote localities.

CHAPTER IX.

HAZELTON TO NAAS.

Routes to the Coast—A Chinook Vocabulary useful—Skirting a Frozen River—Kitsigeuhle—Unpromising Quarters—A Greasy Caravan—Kitwangar Valley—Kitwancole—Pagan Orgies—Ingenious Carving—An Indian Mart—Lake Scenery—Welpamtoots—Valley of the Chean-howan—Trail lost—Muskeeboo—"Yorkshire" Indian—A Trying Walk—Naas Scenery—Alaska visible—Indian Suspension Bridge—Beyond the Chean-howan Canon—Valuable Silver Lode—Basaltic Columns—A Native Bal Masque—Kitawn.

WHILE at the Forks I had many conversations with the miners about the different routes to the coast. One and all spoke very unfavourably of the Skeena, which, in its entire course to the sea passes through a rough and mountainous country. For some distance to where the Killoosâh River enters it, (probably some sixty miles below the Forks) practicable, and in some cases, level benches occur, but below, when the Cascade and Coast ranges intervene, the Skeena flows through deep and rocky canons, where advance by land is extremely difficult and sometimes impossible. As for Port Essington itself, it was described as a miserable swamp, backed by precipitous mountains, and having a shoal and poor harbour, a visit to which would have ill repaid me for the expensive and tedious journey down the Skeena. After having given due consideration, therefore, to the Kitimat route, one which would have brought me to the coast at a more southern point than Port Essington, I decided to cross the country between the Skeena and the Naas, by the latter descend to the sea, where, at its mouth I was informed a good harbour was to be found.

On the 14th of January I took my departure from Hazelton, accompanied by four coast Indians, who engaged with me for the trip at the very moderate rate of seventy-five cents per day. As a matter of course we were provided with snow-shoes, and took a plentiful stock of flour, bacon, beans, tea and dried salmon—the latter, much superior in size and quality to that caught in the more inland waters of Lakes Stewart and Babine. Tom Hankin and McK—— proposed to accompany us for a short distance; so after bidding adieu to the miners we started at three, p.m., following the ice on the Skeena. Six miles below Hazelton I camped, Tom and McK.—returning homeward. My new men were perfect strangers to me, and unable to speak one word of English. They were, however, masters of the Chinook jargon, a vocabulary of which elegant language I carried with me, and by its aid I was soon upon a good understand-

ing with my companions. I had provided a small
cotton tent open at one end. This we usually put up
in front of the fire, and found it extremely convenient; the nights rarely passing without a slight fall
of snow, the disagreeable effects of which this thin
and light covering completely obviated. The next
morning, after breakfast, the men packed up and commenced the journey in good earnest. I gave them a
two hours start, and then followed in their tracks.
Our way lay along the marginal ice of the Skeena,
which was generally open in the middle, and extremely rapid. Now and again when the river
widened, and an interval of slack water was reached;
the ice extended from shore to shore, but this was of
rare occurrence; and from one bank to the other it
was often piled up in the most fantastic shapes,
under which the fierce current rushed and gurgled.
In these cases we were obliged to take to the rocks,
and often had to pass through the thick willows and
underbrush which lined the shore. East of this
morning's camp, and distant five miles, the Rocher
Deboule range could still be seen towering high
above the wide stretch of level benches which intervene between it and the Skeena. About noon as we
made more southing, the same range began to break
away towards the south-east, in which direction a
large valley could be traced for a great distance,
while a mile or so to the south another high range
of mountains trended to the westward as far as the

eye could reach. During the afternoon we passed the Indian Village of Kitsigeuhlé situated on the left bank. This ranche was quite deserted, its usual occupants being then away at a great feast given by the Indians of Kitwancole, a village lying on our route which we expected to reach in a day or two.

A little below Kitsigeuhlé I came upon my Indians as they were resting against a huge fallen spruce; all eyes were turned upon the "Doctor," the most intelligent of the lot, as I came up, and he greeted me in "Chinook": "Cloosh spose nisika sleep;" at the same time pointing to a recess in the steep and densely wooded slopes of the high mountains, which there closed in the left bank of the Skeena. This extraordinary sentence meant that there was a camping place, and that if I did not follow his advice we might go further and fare worse. So I assented, and with a grin of approbation they pitched off their loads, and went to work with alacrity to construct a camp. I must confess that it was not without certain misgivings that I assented, for the spot chosen for our night's resting-place was of forbidding aspect, and did not offer sufficient level space for a dog to coil up in; however, we cleared away the snow down to the very boulders, with which the shore was strewn in great profusion. Immediately above high water mark, the mountain slopes commenced, at an angle of 60° or 70°, while the dense woods and thick underbrush effectually barred their ascent. Here we scratched and dug, filling up holes with boulders and logs, and adding brush, which supplied a carpeting, if not as elegant, at least as comfortable as the finest Brussels. After a couple of hours' steady work the place had undergone quite a transformation, and soon a cheerful fire, in front of which our cotton tent was nicely pitched, lighted up the weird and picturesque scene. At seven the following morning the men were up and away before dawn. For three miles and a half we still kept the ice of the Skeena, when reaching the head of a rapid, we struck to the right, and ascended a steep hill, keeping a nor'west course for the Kitwangar River, which we came to at one p.m., having cut off a good sized triangular piece of the rough country between it and the Skeena.

Since we left the river we met many of the Kitsigeuhlé Indians returning from the great feast at Kitwancole; more than one hundred must have passed us, and they were, without a single exception, not only the men, but also the women and children, laden with large cedar boxes, of the size and shape of tea-chests, which were filled with the rendered grease of the candle fish caught in the Naas waters. What from the rancid and putrescent smell of the grease, and their own filthy persons, down which the perspiration rolled as they plodded laboriously along, bent double in some cases under the crushing weight of their enormous loads, they could, especially when to windward, be scented from afar.

Eight out of every ten of them were suffering from ophthalmia. They passed us in twos and threes; sometimes a whole family, father, mother, and olive branches, all loaded to their utmost capacity; little children even, of tender years, carried burthens of thirty or forty pounds weight, and tottered along in silence. One sturdy savage had, in addition to the usual load of grease, perched on its summit, an old and decrepid woman, perhaps his mother. This man could not have had less than two hundred and fifty pounds weight upon his back; but they are a tough, hardy set, and great carriers.

At three, p.m., we camped amid some spruce trees Since we took the land to-day, we had kept generally at an elevation of seven or eight hundred feet above the Skeena, of which the direction, though itself hidden from view, could be traced by a high and precipitous range of escarped mountains trending far to the west. The snow, which averaged a depth of only fourteen inches, did not trouble us, and was trodden hard by the Indians we had passed. Close to ours was a large camp of Indians returning to their ranche at the mouth of the Kitwangar river.

The days were now excessively short, and daylight had barely appeared at seven, a.m., on the morning of the 7th, when we were again on the road, still benefiting by a fine trail, where we could dispense with our snow-shoes. We were now following up the eastern slope of the Kitwangar valley, which was very rough, and intersected by numerous gullies. The trail kept from a mile to a mile and a half from the river, and soon entered a dense forest of heavy spruce and pine, through which we plodded until ten, when the trail turned suddenly riverwards, and we descended to a beautiful level, in the middle of which the Kitwangar flowed southwards to the Skeena, then distant probably twelve miles. Just before leaving the high ground above, we passed through the centre of an immense encampment of Indians, numbering, at least, two hundred. They paid no attention to us, and we returned the compliment, giving them the "cut direct." Before running the gauntlet of one of those camps we usually broke off stout sticks from some neighbouring tree, with which to repel the too inquisitive and impertinent advances of the Indian dogs, which invariably paid us more attention than their masters, and whose name was legion. Following for three miles the fine level and alluvial bottom, which is from half to three-quarters of a mile wide and about ten feet above the river (a beautiful salmon stream which myriads of those fish annually ascend to the Kitwancole lake), we arrived at Kitwancole, a village of about twenty large houses, situated on the edge of the river, and hemmed in to the east and west by high mountains. The valley which lies north and south is here about a couple of miles in width, and its western slopes are thickly timbered for a long distance up. Notwithstanding the large numbers of Indians whom we had met during this forenoon's march, there were still many at the village. The news of our arrival spreading like wild-fire, there was a general rush of men, women and children from the houses; a large and noisy crowd, disfigured by paint and charcoal, and still bearing the traces of their horrible and disgusting orgies, surrounding and questioning us as to our intent and business. The filth of this heathenish throng was something dreadful, while the abominable stench of the candle fish grease, which they devour in the most inordinate quantities, completely saturated the atmosphere.

My attention was attracted by several tall and stately spars, beautifully carved into the most hideous and fantastic forms of creatures impossible to designate. One of recent construction, and measuring, I should think, four feet at the butt, had just been erected; for the large hole dug to receive it had not yet been filled up. This was the finest I had seen up to the present, and would be worthy of a place in the British Museum. The doors of several of the houses were guarded on each side by large carvings of dogs and other animals, which added to the incongruity of the scene. For the last ten days this village had been the place of barter between the Naas Indians and those of the interior. The former had carried up grease to the extent of many hundred boxes, which they had exchanged with the Skeena Indians for blankets and other articles. Their business being satisfactorily arranged, they wound up by a big "spree," in which, liquor being wanting, they feasted on dried salmon and grease, and danced themselves into a state of prostration from which they were only now recovering.

After a short delay we hurried forward, and following the level valley for several miles, camped about three miles from the outlet of the lake, and twenty-six from Skeena. The next morning, an hour's smart walking over an almost dead level prairie bottom, about half-a-mile in width, brought us to the outlet of the lake, which is about seven miles in length, and lies nearly south-east and north-west. Either side of this picturesque sheet of water is available for a road, but the eastern shore is the better. Hitherto, from the Skeena, our general direction had been nearly due north, but the valley now began to trend nor'-nor'-westerly, and on reaching the upper end of the lake the vista in that direction extended for many miles. To the south-east, the high, snow-capped mountain, which was conspicuous to the westward from Hazelton, appeared to tower far above us to the right, while on the west side the valley was still bounded by a high wall of mountains which stretched north-westerly as far as the eye could reach.

Beyond the upper end of the lake the land was

low and swampy, supporting a fair growth of cedars, and some distance up, on the western slopes of the valley, a little stream came tumbling down through the cedar swamp, until within a mile of the lake, when it seemed to change its mind, and instead of contributing its tiny volume to the waters of the Skeena, turned suddenly round in the opposite direction to add its quota to the Naas. We dined on this watershed, a keen frost giving zest to the dried salmon which the "Doctor" cooked, and served very simply, by quickly presenting, first one side then the other, to the blazing fire, and placing the savoury brown mass upon a chip, a most excellent substitute for a plate. While at dinner several of the Naas Indians overtook and passed us on their way home. They rarely stopped to speak, generally passing on without exhibiting the obtrusive curiosity characteristic of the Indians on the east side of the Rocky Mountains.

Resuming our march after dinner, the trail being yet well beaten, and keeping the slopes in order to avoid the long grass in the low bottom, we passed, three miles and a-half further on, the Indian village of Welpamtoots, and camped two miles lower down the valley. During this afternoon's walk the snow was about two feet in depth. The valley of the Chean-howan, which we had been following since dinner, was here about half-a-mile wide, sometimes stretching out to a greater extent, and perfectly uniform, with a gentle descent towards the Naas of about one in one hundred and twenty. The little river which meandered from side to side of this narrow bottom had cut out a channel from twenty to twenty-five yards in width, and six to eight feet in depth. In places its bed was almost dry, and strewn with small boulders.

This valley had a most singular appearance; the narrow level portion, between the mountain slopes, was so perfectly uniform that it seemed as if some giant had planed it, while the surface bore a luxuriant crop of grass, with occasionally a clump of cedars, spruce, or immense rough-bark poplars. The river margin was covered with a dense thicket of willows, which rendered walking extremely difficult. Our camp was situated some seventy feet above the river, and was quite unsheltered. We had, however, abundance of dry wood; and the night not being cold, we slept comfortably, and were on our way betimes the following morning. The barometer dropped 4-10ths of an inch since last evening, and snow had fallen steadily during the greater part of the night, which rendered travelling this forenoon very fatiguing. We pushed on, however, the trail becoming very much worse, the barometer falling steadily, and a constant drizzle of fine hard snow totally obscuring the mountains. After making poor progress we camped near a large assemblage of Naas Indians, who were returning homewards.

Here the trail, or what was left of it, disappeared entirely, and we had now to beat the road through three feet of snow, very soft, and extremely difficult to plough through. We were joined by one of the Indians at this place, who kept us company, and good-naturedly took his turn at beating the road. This individual bore the name of "Muskeeboo." He was a chief in his way, and professed a knowledge of the English language; but he spoke with a strong Yorkshire accent, very difficult to understand. We were now fairly in for a spell of very heavy walking, there being no trail; the cunning Nascars carefully keeping in the rear, in order to benefit by our track, which now lay through thick brush, and sometimes crossing the Chean-howan on the ice, as it interrupted our line of travel.

On the 11th, at noon, after having followed the high banks on the right side of the river for some distance, we again struck the Chean-howan, and camped upon its banks. Here we were overtaken by a Nascar chief, who, with his deaf and dumb nephew, was on his way to Kitlatamox, a village situated on the Naas, about twenty-five miles above tide-water. The snow was now fully three and a half feet deep, and extremely soft, causing us great labour in beating the road. The front man had no sinecure, as at every step, even with large snow-shoes, he sank down a couple of feet. Muskeeboo and I, therefore, took our turn in the van, changing our position every few hundred yards; and although the thermometer stood at about zero, we were glad to strip off our superfluous clothing, and walk in our shirt-sleeves. Even in this light costume, half-an-hour of such laborious work sufficed to bring out the perspiration in beads, which coursed down our faces, and occasioned intense thirst among us all, to allay which the Indians scooped up, now and again, a handful of snow, which they consumed with evident relish. On the 12th, at noon, we stopped for dinner on the side of a high hill overhanging the river; and while the men were making a fire, and melting snow for our tea-water, Muskeeboo and I ascended the hill, to obtain a view of the country to the south-west, in which direction lay Kitlatamox. We were obliged to furnish ourselves with long poles, without which the ascent would have been impossible. As it was, half-an-hour was occupied in getting up to an altitude of four hundred feet above our fire; but from that position we had a famous view of the country for many miles. The hills on the west side of the Naas could be seen very distinctly, and the far-off snow-capped mountains of Alaska peeped up here and there in the blue distance. Six hundred feet below, the little Chean-howan trickled on over its gravelly bed, which, in the summer season, is the haunt of many a lusty salmon. The valley at this point was about nine hundred yards wide, and thickly timbered with extremely large rough-bark poplar, spruce, birch, and a species of red pine, which grew to a large size. When descending the hill-side, which was entirely bereft of timber, and in some places covered with snow to a depth of four feet, a slip occurred, which, however, had only the effect of startling us. Several score of Indians overtook us to-day; but on reaching our fire, they stopped, coolly intimating their intention to wait for our track. We accordingly pushed on, after anathematizing the lazy rascals in no measured terms; and following the river for some distance, took the right bank of the valley, and camped amongst a dense grove of pine and balsam, the latter furnishing fine bedding upon which to lay our blankets—the cunning dogs of Nascars, who clung to us like limpets to a rock, camping beside us.

On the 13th, at six, a.m., we moved on; a mile and a-half over the hills taking us to the edge of the valley again, down the sides of which we slid for about two hundred and fifty feet, and as the day was breaking, reached the bed of the Chean-howan, close to an Indian suspension bridge. The uniform and even bottom, through which the river had found its way from the watershed, now disappeared entirely, giving place to a deep and rocky gully, the rugged walls of which rose perpendicularly for a hundred feet on either side, as we picked our way laboriously over huge fragments of dolerite which strewed the river bed. At eight, a.m., we emerged from the darkness of the Chean-howan Canon, and took the ice on the Naas, here not more than sixty yards wide, and walled in by perpendicular trap rocks, one hundred and fifty feet in height. We had now good ice, and travelled for five miles, until we reached the head of a series of rapids, when we took the land, and stopped to rest and boil the kettle. Although we were able to keep the ice since leaving the Chean-howan, walking was very laborious, the snow being deep, and saturated with water from the overflowings. At dinner, we were rejoined by our pertinacious friends, the Nascars, who came up as we were leaving the fire. Ascending the left bank of the Naas, of which we now lost sight altogether, as it coursed on towards the sea through a canon two hundred and fifty feet in depth, we made our way through dense woods, and camped, after making about fifteen miles, and breaking the trail through three and a-half feet of snow.

At nine the following morning we descended again to the river by a winding and precipitous path, where the utmost caution had to be used, taking the ice three hundred and fifty feet below the trail, and about ten miles below the head of the rapids. A mile and a-half further, we passed a little river coming from the Nor'-West, upon which there is reported to be a large and valuable silver ode. We had now good ice for about seven miles, until another rapid caused us to take the woods for a short distance; and after clambering over a rocky point, we again took the river on a narrow ledge of ice, two feet wide, upon which we very cautiously crawled for two hundred yards, having, on one hand, a perpendicular wall of rock, while, on the other, the swift waters of the Naas seethed and boiled in a manner which actually caused the blood to curdle, as a single false step would have inevitably cost us our lives. A quarter of a mile below this rapid we passed some very extraordinary columnar basaltic rocks, of which the river banks were composed; but night coming on, and there being every indication of a heavy snow fall, I had no time to examine minutely their curious appearance. Following Muskeeboo, who now took the lead, we walked on for three miles more, and put up in that gentleman's ranche at Kitlatamox, where we arrived at half-past five.

Kitlatamox is a large village, situated on the banks of the Naas, and about twenty-five miles from tide-water. It has a population of about three hundred, who subsist entirely on the salmon and other fish which frequent this river in myriads. Muskeeboo's house, unlike *all* the others, was passably clean, and his family—a large one—bestirred themselves to make things comfortable for my accommodation. The house was what we would call, in the civilized world, a tenement, there being another distinct family on the ground floor, while

Muskeeboo occupied the upper portion, to which access was obtained from the outside by stairs. Muskeeboo's portion consisted of one large room, forty feet by sixty, in the centre of which was a large square space, covered with earth, on which some blazing logs barely sufficed to give the necessary warmth, and to light up the immediate neighbourhood of the fireplace, around which were grouped about a dozen specimens of aborigines. Sundry chests of rendered "uhlihan" grease, and dried salmon in great quantities, were piled up against the walls, which were boarded with hewn pine planks thirty inches wide. Enormous beams supported the low flat roof, open above the fireplace, to allow the acrid smoke to escape. In addition to his ordinary avocations, Muskeeboo did a small business in groceries, which he disposed of to the other Indians, in consideration of certain furs, such as martens, foxes, etc., etc.,—a barrel or two of biscuits and Sandwich Island sugar being his stock-in-trade.

Nine miles below the village, and on the same side of the river, there is another large ranche called Kitwanshelt, for which we started on the 16th, having been detained by bad weather; snow and rain having fallen without intermission during the whole of the day before. There were three or four miners at Kitlatamox, then on their way to the Forks of Skeena. They had recently arrived from Fort Simpson, and were awaiting the return of the Indians from Kitwancole in order to benefit by their trail. One of them proposed, to accompany me to McNeil's, at the mouth of the Naas, so he and I, together with Muskeeboo, left the village at noon, and after following the ice for the greater part of the way, reached Kitwanshelt at half-past three, in the midst of a fearful down-pour of rain. During the greater part of this distance the banks were rather low, and four miles below the upper village on the left bank we passed a small river coming from the eastward. This stream flowed through a fine open valley, walled in on the south by the Cascade range, which we were now entering. This valley, Muskeeboo informed me, afforded an excellent route to the Skeena, upon which it debouches above the Kitsellasse Canon. The bottom of this valley, as also that of an immense flat extending for several miles below the outlet of the little stream, was composed of scoriæ, probably the result of ancient volcanic disturbance. The mountains about here were extremely rugged, and densely timbered for a long way up, but were much obscured by the heavy mists which hung over them. On reaching the village, Muskeeboo conducted me to a large house owned by a friend of his, where I found my men already quartered, they having preceded me by a few hours. This village is situated upon a rocky point overhanging the river, and consists of, probably, a score of houses.

During the course of the evening, and after supper, we were entertained by the exhibition of a native dance, in which some fifty men and women participated. They came trooping in, nearly all masked and dressed in the most curious attire; the men divested of their nether garments, and the women rather scantily arrayed, considering the time of the year. To describe the dance would be impossible. The motions were vigorous; and if not graceful, were, at any rate, whimsical, and rather free; the men and women dancing alternately. There seemed to be a leader on each side, who did his or her utmost to execute the most fantastic steps, which were accompanied by frightful facial contortions, and a monotonous chant, with which they kept excellent time. After an hour's exhibition they desisted, and retired to their respective habitations, completely worn out, as indeed they well might be, their antics having been more like those of a band of escaped lunatics than of rational beings. During the intervals of the dance I examined some of the masks, which were beautifully made. They were of all styles, and represented the faces of different animals. I was much struck with one, a delicately carved wooden imitation of an eagle's head, with a rather exaggerated beak and movable eyes, which, during the most vigorous part of the dance, rolled about in a manner fearful to contemplate. The house now being quiet, I made my bed in one of the many vacant bunks built against the walls, and soon the steady pattering of the rain without was the only sound to be heard in the now sleeping village.

The next morning, on getting up, it was still pouring, and a thick, heavy mist hung over the valley, completely hiding the Cascade range which we had now to enter and pass through before reaching the "salt-chuck" (sea), which was yet about eighteen miles distant. The unusual comfort of the ranche had caused us to oversleep ourselves, so that by the time breakfast was over, and our traps were packed, it was ten o'clock before we were fairly on our way again. We were obliged to put on our snow-shoes, there being no trail, and the snow lying fully four feet deep along the river margin and on the thickly timbered flats which now extended for half a mile or more back from the river. As we had anticipated, the walking was now execrable, as the snow was saturated with rain, and water covered the ice to a depth of several inches. In many places the river was quite open, obliging us to keep the right bank, as we were unable to cross to the opposite side. Our progress was consequently very slow, and at dusk we were still a long way from the Indian village of Kitawn, which lay a few miles below tide-water. We still walked on through a steady down-pour of rain, and reached the ranche at nine p.m., completely drenched and our snow-shoes entirely used up from the effects of the water through which we had been obliged to wade for the last ten miles.

On our arrival we very unceremoniously entered one of the houses, and, rousing up the inmates, a fire was speedily lighted, by which we dried ourselves. The master of this establishment was excessively affable and accommodating, and furnished clean cedar mats, on which we stretched ourselves before the fire, where we slept until morning. Nothing could be more dismal than the aspect of affairs on the following day, the 18th January, when I got up and went outside to look around. The rain still continued, and a dense, impenetrable mist hung over the houses and the river, completely obscuring the nearest objects; and although the high mountains of the Cascade range towered above in our immediate vicinity, we might have been in the midst of the prairie, for aught we could tell to the contrary. After breakfast we crossed on the ice to McNeil's establishment, about a mile distant, and which until recently belonged to the Hudson Bay Company, who have now entirely abandoned their posts on this river.

CHAPTER X.

NAAS TO FORT SIMPSON.

Detained by Rain—Hazardous Canoeing—Camping on the Sea Coast—Geographical Outlines—Salmon Cove—Observatory Inlet—An Avalanche—Naas Harbour—South Inlet—A Critical Five Minutes—Work Channel—Chimsean Peninsula—Birnie Island—Arrival at Fort Simpson—The Harbour—American Military Post—Moral and Religious Condition of the Indians—Canoe Building—Agricultural Facilities.

AT NAAS I paid off my Indians and set about engaging a crew and canoe to take me to Fort Simpson. I was detained, however, until the 20th, not being able to procure Indians except at the most exorbitant figures, and it was only after considerable difficulty that McNeil and I were enabled to induce the necessary number to engage for the trip, which at this season promised to be very disagreeable and perhaps hazardous. In the meantime, on the afternoon of the 18th, heavy rain again set in, and the dreary fog, which during the forenoon of the same day had partially lifted, settled down yet lower than before, entirely putting an end to the hopes I had entertained of seeing the nature of the mountains which lie in the rear of McNeil's miserable shanty. The rain poured in torrents, and found its way through many a chink and hole in the weather-beaten roof of the little house, which lay back some little way from the river, and was surrounded by high willows.

On the 20th, having managed to hire eight men and a very fine canoe, we started down the river for the open water, which was yet six miles distant. The snow had partially melted away, and six inches of water lay upon the ice, through which we waded with the utmost unconcern, for use soon renders one callous to little inconveniences of this kind. The canoe was mounted on a roughly-constructed sled, and all hands, aided by some supernumerary assistants, "tailing on," we made steady progress to the edge of the ice, which we reached as the tide was on the turn of flood. The day having been nearly spent in getting away from the house, I determined on camping, as there was every indication of a heavy blow and more bad weather. We accordingly stopped on a little flat piece of ground, close to the water's edge, where the remains of some scaffolding, used the previous summer for fish-curing purposes, supplied us with the scanty means of making a fire. Two of us set to work to clear away the snow, four feet deep, with our snow-shoes, while the others made off to some distant green timber for brush and additional firewood. I found camp-making on the sea-coast, and in the midst of a pelting rain, a very different affair from the same operation in the interior, and oh! how I wished for a temperature of twenty degrees or thirty degrees below zero. The snow was of course saturated and very heavy, and the labour of clearing a space large enough to accommodate us all was by no means light. As we cleared down to the ground little rills of water trickled in all directions, presenting but a poor prospect for a dry night's lodging. My men, however, brought down several good loads of green brush, which we spread on the wet ground, and rigging the cotton tent and sails by the aid of the masts and paddles, we managed to protect ourselves to a great extent from the fury of the winter storm which burst upon us as we were putting the finishing strokes to our encampment.

It was now four, p.m., and perfectly dark, the barometer had sunk to twenty-nine inches, but the temperature was high comparatively, the thermometer standing at thirty-five degrees Fah't. There had been little wind all day, but now the storm-king began to assert his power, and heavy gusts followed each other in rapid succession, driving the pitiless rain, which soon changed to sleet and snow, in our faces, and on one occasion carrying off our tent and sails bodily into the river. With great difficulty we started a fire, and having again secured our cotton shelter in the best manner possible, passed the long and weary hours as pleasantly as could be expected under the circumstances. Every now and then some sudden and terrific gust would sweep down the valley, and threaten to blow fire, tent and everything into the water; the acrid smoke produced blew in eddies, and almost blinded us, while the snow and sleet beat upon our frail covering, which, not being of the very best quality, leaked, and caused a constant drip, drip, which we could have very thankfully dispensed with. Under such circumstances, a good night's rest was out of the question, and we hailed the tardy morning light with undisguised pleasure.

At eight a.m. on the 21st, the glass had gone up to 29·80 inches, the wind had quite calmed down, and the clouds breaking, gave us the promise of a short "spell" of fine weather. We accordingly packed up and launched our canoe, which was made of cedar, a "dug-out" in fact, but shaped in a most graceful mould, and evidently intended to stand a rough sea. Embarking at nine we paddled towards the Salmon Cove, distant six miles and a-half. The traces of last night's storm had almost entirely disappeared, and the sky was nearly clear, a few vapoury clouds still clinging about the mountains, which I now had the opportunity of seeing properly for the first time. Opposite our camp the river was a mile and a-half wide; very high mountains rose from the water edge on both sides, and a mile below camp there was barely room to land, the steep, slippery rocks rising almost perpendicularly from the water, and offering no chance for any creature less sure-footed than a goat. The scenery was grand, but fearfully desolate. The wind having entirely gone down, the long, powerful strokes of my Indian crew urged our clipper-modelled craft through the smooth water with a noiselessness and speed difficult to realize. Now and again we stopped to enjoy the different phases of the scenery, as each succeeding point revealed some fresh portion of the panorama; presently we opened out the Salmon Cove, which now lay to our left. A little further on, we caught sight of the few houses of the English Church Mission station, which bore from us nor'-west, and was fully three miles distant. We had now also an unobstructed view of the land on the west side of Observatory Inlet, and could just see Point Ramsden, distant seven miles. The Naas Entrance, opposite the mission station, is about one mile and a-half wide, and there is a fair anchorage in five and seven fathoms, abreast of the Mission-house. With but one or two exceptions, the shores were steep and almost impracticable, and snow-clad mountains rose on every hand to an altitude of four or five thousand feet, presenting an endless view of surpassing beauty and rugged grandeur. The beautiful bay in which we now were, is sometimes the scene of terrific storms, which generally blow either from the east or west. The easterly winds are by far the worst, although coming from inland. Their violence is something terrific, sweeping down, as they do, along the high Cascade range, the deep and narrow gap through which the Naas finds its way to the sea, forming a funnel which the winds rush through with a violence that nothing can withstand. We were in luck, however, the wind being, to use a sailor's expression, right " up and down," the mirror-like surface of the deep blue waters of the Pacific reflecting with fidelity the surrounding mountains, of which the inverted forms now and again undulated almost imperceptibly, as if in homage to the spent swell of the great ocean beyond.

We were now four and a-half miles from the bottom of Salmon Cove, which lay to the west-sou'-west. On our port hand was a small level flat covered, like the mountains above it, with heavy timber. East of this a narrow defile appeared to offer the only available means of communication with the interior from this harbour, which is none of the best, one drawback being the existence of an immense mud-bank extending a long distance out from the flat alluded to, which offers the only convenient site on which a village could be built. Three-quarters of a mile out lies a small dark wooded island, and half-a-mile further to the sou'-west, another. While paddling along gently, we saw an avalanche occur down one of the high mountains to the eastward; this phenomenon must be of rather frequent occurrence in this mountainous neighbourhood. The one we saw took place about two miles off, and even at that distance, the noise of the immense mass of snow, as it slid bodily down the mountain slope, and over a high precipice on to the trees below, where it cleared an avenue for itself in a twinkling, could be heard quite distinctly. My Indians watched the incident with great delight, exclaiming, when it was all over: "Hiu snow! Hiu snow!" Several more avalanches, but on a smaller scale, were witnessed by us, and we finally paddled up to the end of the bay, where we landed at noon.

I now determined to send the canoe round to the Nasoga Inlet, a *détour* of at least twenty miles, while I and a couple of Indians were to camp here, and make the portage the following day. Before the canoe left, we boiled our kettle and lunched on tea and dried salmon. Pending the preparations, I got out my photographic apparatus, and succeeded in getting a negative of the bay, which must be lovely in the summer season, but at this time (21st January) was cold and gloomy, snow lying on the ground to a depth of three feet. Reserving for ourselves blankets and provisions for a couple of days, the canoe pushed off, and we set about making the last camp but one of the season. Mr. T.'s Mission Station was now hidden by the projecting point at the entrance of the cove, but its bearing was about north by east, and the distance five miles. I did not derive much pleasure from this examination of the Naas Harbour; but after all, when the barren and rugged nature of the country which I had just passed over is taken into consideration, the absence of a really good and safe harbour is hardly to be deprecated. If, however, the Omenica gold mines should ever become valuable, I have no doubt that communication between them and the coast may be eventually established *via* the Naas, in order to avoid the Skeena route, which, at best, is a bad one. There may yet be an easier way to reach the interior. From the head of the east arm of Observatory Inlet the distance to the Naas River is not over twenty miles, and, by Indian reports, trail making between these two points would not be difficult. If such be the case, the difficulties of the Naas River would be avoided, and a road would cross that river at or near the Chean-howan, whence the Forks of Skeena could be reached in a distance of seventy-five miles, thus bringing Hazelton within ninety-five miles of the Pacific. This would involve the construction of twenty-five miles of road from Kitwancole Lake, in an east-south-east direction, to the Forks, opposite which it would debouch. The portion here alluded to has not yet been travelled by white men, but the Indians say there are no difficulties in the way of a pack trail. Hardly had the canoe disappeared behind the point, when the sky again became overcast, and at three, p.m. a steady fall of snow set in. As the night wore on, the weather became squally, and strong gusts from the northward occasioned us no small anxiety regarding the safety of the canoe, which had to pass several miles of open and perfectly iron-bound coast, where to land was impossible. We, however, consoled ourselves with the reflection that the men knew what they were about, and arriving at the conclusion that they had not gone beyond the last haven of refuge, we turned in for the night. At three, a.m., of the 22nd, the aneroids reached their lowest readings, while terrific squalls from the nor'ard shook the trees under which we had pitched our tent, fanning the dying embers of our fire into flames, and scattering the red-hot cinders in a manner dangerous to the safety of our cotton tent, which already bore the marks of many a stormy night's bivouac. At 8.45 we started on our way across the portage to the head of Nasoga Inlet. The distance, as the crow flies, is only two miles, but owing to the depth and clogginess of the snow, saturated as it was after the late heavy rains, our progress was slow. We followed a little salmon stream for a mile, sometimes through a perfect network of willows, ascending and descending ravines of no mean depth, and when about half over we had to fell a couple of trees, upon which we crossed the brawling little creek. Finally, after three hours' walking of the most fatiguing kind through a dense forest, we reached the other end, and descended to the beach at the head of the south inlet. The canoe had not yet made its appearance, so we prepared to camp; an immense stranded red cedar, at least five feet in diameter, supplying us with firewood ready to hand. We accordingly pitched our tent just beyond the reach of the incoming tide, placing layers of brush on the wet beach, on which to sleep. While occupied with the details of camping, a couple of sea lions made their appearance close in shore. My Indians fired several ineffectual shots at them, but the brutes dived simultaneously with the flashes of the gun, and bobbing up again in some other unexpected spot, seemed to laugh at our futile attempts. At four, p.m., the canoe arrived; the men had been obliged to put ashore shortly after leaving the Salmon Cove, and had not left until very late, on account of the heavy sea running outside. They had been more successful then we, for they had bagged a large and fine seal, portions of which they soon had in the pot, and they devoured nearly the whole before morning. By nine, p.m., it had completely calmed down again; the sky had also cleared, but the glass fell steadily until five, a.m., of the 23rd, when a light breeze sprung up from the nor'-nor'-east. At seven, a.m., we embarked, and paddled beyond the shelter of the high land we had crossed on the previous day, when hoisting the foresail, we sped down the inlet at the rate of six miles per hour. We soon found ourselves in a pretty heavy sea, over which our brave little craft careered in beautiful style. On emerging from the inlet we found a heavy swell setting in from the north, and continuing along the iron-bound coast we put ashore at noon in a sandy bay, to boil the kettle and warm ourselves, for the weather was chilly, the thermometer having stood at thirty-two degrees during the whole forenoon.

Since we left the inlet, we had passed only two or three places where there was any possibility of landing, the shores being almost invariably steep and inaccessible, while mountains upon mountains were clustered together in endless variety of form. Occasionally, a deep inlet could be seen, until lost to view in the intricacies of the mountains on our left, while numerous islands, of large extent, protected the inner channel we had taken from the effects of the angry swell outside, of which we occasionally caught a glimpse. For ruggedness, this coast cannot have its equal. To walk from the Naas to Fort Simpson (whither we were now bound), would be a perfect impossibility, owing to the numerous inlets and bays, and the impassable character of the ground. The whole coast, down to Cape Caution, has much the same appearance, and is, if anything, worse.

Starting again, we paddled westward for four miles through a narrow channel, the width of which barely averaged half-a-mile. On the north side, we had a high mountainous island, and on our left, the rugged shores of the mainland, which we hugged very closely. Opening out Dundas Island, which lay sixteen miles to the west and south, we reached a rocky headland, at the base of which the seas were running fearfully high, the wind having veered to north, and now blowing a gale. Before going any further, a consultation was held as to the feasibility of attempting this short but hazardous piece of navigation, and, after a little while, it was decided to risk it. The foremast was accordingly stepped, the sail reefed, sheet hauled aft in readiness; and after seeing everything clear (which my men did in a seamanlike manner), we paddled out for a short distance, in order to clear the eddies caused by the high island immediately to windward. All hands being now stationed in their respective places, in order to help with the paddles, we put the helm "up," our cedar "dug-out" obeying the impulse immediately, and away we bounded over the seething waters at a fearful rate. The captain and another steered and handled their large paddles with the most consummate skill, and the way in which the beautiful little vessel answered her helm, as the steersman laid her broadside on in the immense hollows, down which we every now and again disappeared, was wonderful. As we rose from the trough of the sea, off she paid again, assisted by the united efforts of the paddlers, flying through the hissing waves like a thing of life, sometimes for an instant hesitating, as we rushed up the side of a solid wall of water, and again, gathering fresh impetus, dashing madly down the next huge billow, the long projecting bow dipping under alarmingly. Five minutes of this exciting work took us again into comparatively smooth water, where we rested for a few minutes to light up the tobacco pipe, the inseparable companion of the *voyageur*. The canoe and its burthen now presented rather a curious appearance, the spray and water we had shipped speedily evaporating under the cheering influence of the sun, which had now made its appearance, left everything coated with a thick layer of sea salt.

Three miles further, we sighted the Work Channel, or "Canal," as it is sometimes called. This is an arm of the sea, which extends inland in a south-easterly direction for thirty-five miles. It has a width of from one to two miles, and terminates within three-quarters of a mile of the right or north bank of the Skeena, to which access can be had from this direction, by a short but rough portage of less than a mile in length. Still keeping on for a few miles, we rounded the north-west point of the Chimsean Peninsula; and running in between the mainland and Birnie Island, caught sight of the now welcome Fort, where the rough and disagreeable portion of our journey was to terminate. From Birnie Island to the Fort was but three miles, which we soon accomplished, and our tight little craft grounded on the muddy beach at the Fort precisely at four, p.m. Several miners, on their way to the Omenica, *via* the Naas, curious to find out who we were, stood on the beach where we landed, and in answer to their inquiry as to where we came from, they received the laconic answer, " Fort Garry." A stare of incredulity was returned, and I hastened on to Mr. Morrison's quarters, where the most cordial welcome awaited me from that gentleman and his wife, whose kindness and attention I shall never forget. My traps being brought up to the Fort, I was soon installed in the most comfortable of quarters, to await the arrival of the Hudson's Bay Company's steamer "Otter," then due on her winter trading voyage. On the following morning, my crew received their pay, which they soon got rid of amongst the many inveterate gamblers of Fort Simpson, who not only fleeced them of the money received for their trip, but also gave them a sound thrashing, probably following out the principle sometimes adopted in more civilized communities of knocking a man down, and then kicking him for falling.

I had been particularly struck with the great decrease in the depth of snow since leaving the Naas, and was very agreeably surprised to find, on my arrival here, perfectly bare ground; but Mr. Morrison told me that here, at no time during the winter, does snow ever lie for any length of time, or to any great depth.

Fort Simpson is in latitude 54 deg. 33 min. north, and longitude 130 deg. 24 min. west. The harbour is an excellent one, and of rather large extent. It is sheltered from the westerly winds by Finlayson Island, and a large reef of outlying rocks. The north-west winds alone can affect it, and these only to a slight degree, while on every other hand it is completely land-locked. In the immediate vicinity, the land is not very high—one or two hills, from eight hundred to fourteen hundred feet in height, in the rear of the Fort, being the most conspicuous points. All around Fort Simpson harbour, the rare and wonderful occurrence of a sandy beach is to be met with, and, I believe, as far as Metlah Catlah, a mission station some eighteen or twenty miles down the coast, the same phenomenon is repeated at intervals. Those are, I believe, the only instances of actual beaches occurring in all the immense extent of iron-bound coast extending from the northern boundary line to Cape Caution, a distance of three hundred nautical miles. There is excellent anchorage within a cable's length of the beach, below the Fort, and vessels can lie there in perfect safety with seven fathoms of water, and good holding ground beneath them. Some forty-five miles north-west of Fort Simpson, is situated the late American military post of Tongas, now abandoned by the troops, whose quarters have been removed to Sitka, the capital of that valuable acquisition of the United States, Alaska. Although deserted by the military, the forsaken wooden shanties of Fort Tongas are still watched over by a civil functionary, and the stars and stripes yet wave above the door of the solitary individual on whom devolve the not very onerous duties of custom-house officer.

In front of Fort Simpson there is an excellent hard and uniform beach, where the American steamer, which used to ply between Portland (Oregon) and Sitka, has been laid up for repairs. The Fort itself belongs to the Hudson's Bay Company, and is built in the form of a quadrangle, flanked at each corner by wooden towers of insignificant pretensions. The dwelling-houses, stores and offices of the Company are inside; and a double entrance-gate, studded with iron, completely cuts off communication with the Indians who live in the immediate neighbourhood. The Indian population here numbers about five hundred souls. Some hundred or more houses of various sizes, but all built upon the same principle, afford shelter to the lazy inhabitants of this village, who, unlike the inland Indians, are never pushed to extremities for the want of food; the Pacific, which washes the very thresholds of their dwellings, affording a never-failing supply of salmon and halibut, besides other fish; while the adjoining beaches are covered with shell-fish, such as clams, cockles and mussels, in endless profusion. The moral character of the Chimsean Indian is decidedly low. In their domestic relations, they are indifferent; and I think it may be said of them generally, that the marriage tie is knotted with a view to being slipped with facility. Attempts have been made to Christianize these Coast savages, but have not been crowned with success, a Christian Indian being usually looked upon with suspicion by the knowing ones among the coast traders. Eighteen or twenty miles from Fort Simpson, a Mr. Duncan, a missionary of the English Church, has established a station for the promulgation of the gospel among the Chimseans; but whether or not his efforts have met with the success they deserve, this deponent knoweth not. According to the best authority, the total population of the Chimsean Peninsula is about fifteen hundred; but pulmonary and other complaints are rapidly reducing the number.

The connoisseur in ship-building might here indulge his fancy to his heart's content; for about the beach and houses, innumerable cedar canoes, of every size, are to be seen, every Indian being generally the owner of one, if not more, of these light and graceful craft. The finest and best canoes are brought from the Queen Charlotte Islands, where the yellow cedar grows to a great size. The Hyders, as the Indians inhabiting those islands are called, excel in many mechanical arts. They carve most beautifully, and some of the specimens of canoe-building cannot be surpassed in graceful appearance, and capabilities for speed. The Chimsean Indians usually purchase those large canoes from the Hyders, who bring them over from their insular home in the early part of the summer, during the prevalence of fine weather. They are sometimes, however, overtaken by sudden storms during the passage to the mainland, when they generally display the greatest skill in handling their comparatively tiny craft. In the art of working such metals as gold, silver and copper into a variety of ornamental articles, they exhibit as much ingenuity and skill as are met with in cities among regularly-trained artizans—some specimens of bracelets, rings, and other articles, which I saw at Fort Simpson, being really well done. In physique, the Hyders are superior to the Indians of the mainland, and in features they bear no slight resemblance to the Japanese, whose descendants they probably are.

There is little land about Fort Simpson available for culture; but the Hudson's Bay Company grow a few vegetables, and, from all accounts, the climate is not too severe, nor are the seasons too short for the raising of cereals.

CHAPTER XI.

FORT SIMPSON TO NANAIMO.

On board the "Otter"—A "played-ont" Boiler—Rose Spit—Graham Island—Masset Harbour—Clams—Mineral Wealth—A Nor'-Easter—Dundas Island—Fort Simpson again—Porcher Island—Arthur Channel—Seaforth—Bella Bella—Dean Channel—Bella Coula—The Old Route to Fraser River—Perilous Anchorage—King Island—Safety Cove—Queen Charlotte Sound—Beaver Harbour—Description of Scenery—Discovery Passage—Alberni Canal—The Canada Pacific Route—Cape Mudge—Port Augusta—Off Nanaimo.

ON THE morning of the 31st January, while still in bed, I was agreeably surprised to hear the familiar sound of a steam-whistle; and on getting up, the waiting-man informed me that the long-looked-for "Otter" had at length made her appearance, and had just dropped anchor in front of the Fort. Presently, Captain Lewis, her commander, came ashore, and informed us that, as soon as the cargo for this place was landed, he would run over to Masset harbour, on the northern island of the Queen Charlotte group. That evening, after bidding farewell to Mr. and Mrs. Morrison, I embarked at eight o'clock, and making my way to the snug cabin of the "Otter, found a berth ready for my use. The next morning, at five o'clock, the rattling of the chain cable, which was soon followed by the peculiar sound of the screw, announced our departure from Fort Simpson. At eight bells, when off the north end of Dundas Island, the steward announced breakfast, to which Captain Lewis, the chief engineer, and I, sat down. On questioning Mr. Elliot, the engineer, regarding our slow rate of speed, he informed me that the boiler now in use had been in the "Otter" for the last twenty years, and was about "played out," so much so, that fourteen lbs. of steam was the maximum allowed, adding that a slight explosion might be expected at any time. The "Otter" was a sound, staunch oak vessel of 200 tons, built in England, and brought out under canvas, *via* Cape Horn. Her captain was a fine old gentleman, who could boast of an almost perfect knowledge of the Pacific coast, from Puget Sound to Sitka. Captain Lewis had the supervision of all the Hudson's Bay Company's posts on the coast, from Victoria upwards, and between that and the navigation of the "Otter" his time was pretty well occupied. We had a splendid day for our voyage, the weather being clear, with a light air from the north-east, which we took advantage of by setting the foresail and mainsail. With the exception of a slight ground swell, the sea was quite calm, while the air, although slightly frosty, was most exhilarating. The thermometer stood at 32 deg. Fahrenheit until ten, a.m., when it rose as the wind veered to the south-west, the barometer then beginning to fall. At one o'clock we were off the Rose Spit, a very dangerous sand stretching far out from the north-eastern extremity of Graham Island, the low wooded shores of which were just beginning to show in the hazy distance. The contrast in the appearance of the mainland and Graham Island was very striking. Astern, and forty miles distant, the cold, bleak and serrated contour of the coast range could be traced from north to south, presenting a most uninviting appearance, while the still more dreary-looking mountains of Alaska intercepted the northern horizon. At three, p.m., we neared the entrance to Masset Harbour, and were soon surrounded by numerous canoes, which came out to meet us. Twenty minutes later, the anchor was let go, abreast of the Indian village, and within two hundred yards of the shore; the passage from Fort Simpson having occupied exactly ten hours.

Masset being a very bad and unsafe anchorage, Captain Lewis at once set to work discharging goods for the use of the Hudson's Bay post here, and taking in, in return, sundry kegs of dog fish oil, skins of the fur seal, and other furs. The harbour here is merely an arm of the sea, about a mile in width, running into the interior of the island for fifteen or twenty miles. Unlike the inlets on the mainland, the banks of this one are very low; and the tide rushing up and down with great velocity, there is sometimes created, with wind from the opposite direction, a very nasty and confused sea, dangerous to vessels lying at anchor. It was for this reason that Captain Lewis was desirous of getting away from this rather unsafe place, and every exertion was accordingly made to hasten our departure. On Sunday, while the steamer's crew and a gang of Hyders were loading up, in anticipation of bad weather, the Captain and I went ashore, to take a stroll through the village, and along the beautiful beach, which extends for many miles along the northern shore of the island. The Indian ranches here were exactly similar in appearance to those on the mainland, and were ornamented, like them, with carvings in wood. Passing east of the village, we entered a forest of fine large timber, and, continuing through it, reached the gravel beach beyond. Traces of a recent storm were yet visible in the huge piles of clams lately thrown up by the surf, and now covering the beach for miles.

Although now in the very heart of winter, the weather was comparatively mild, the thermometer ranging from 36 deg. to 40 deg. Fahrenheit, neither were there more than three inches of snow in the sheltered places, while the rare occurrence of ice was an additional proof of the mildness of the climate.

On the more southern islands of the group, the seasons are even milder; but the country is of a mountainous nature, abounding in mineral wealth—rich and vast deposits of anthracite coal, veins of copper, and, very recently, gold, having been worked to advantage. Yellow cedar and pine are found in large quantities; on the other hand, the soil in many places is well adapted for agriculture. This group of islands is certainly rich in undeveloped wealth, and will at some future day form a very important portion of the British possessions on the Pacific.

Early on the morning of the 4th, a heavy northeast gale, accompanied by rain and snow, set in, preventing our departure for the Skeena, whither we were now bound. We, therefore, remained at anchor all day; but the next morning, at two o'clock, steamed out of Masset Harbour. For three hours we had the advantage of a smooth sea, until just before daylight, when, emerging from the shelter of the island, we met the full force of a stiff south-easter, which kicked up a tremendous sea, and caused the "Otter" to pitch and roll in fine style. Coming on deck as the first faint streaks of dawn were beginning to pierce the gloomy clouds which now covered the entire firmament, a strange and novel scene met my gaze. The little "Otter" was staggering along, close hauled by the wind, under double-reefed fore and mainsails, now and again burying her bows beneath the confused sea, which the conflicting efforts of an ebb tide and southerly gale had now raised. Captain Lewis, who was executing a sort of double-shuffle on the slippery deck, in answer to my inquiry as to when we should reach the Skeena, shook his head:—"No Skeena for us this day! I'm afraid we shall have to bear up for Fort Simpson yet," said he, casting a critical look around the troubled expanse of waters; "this beggarly wind is hauling more to the eastward, and we can't fetch the passage." In fact, we were now heading north-east by north, a course which, had we been making no lee-way, would have taken us to the yet unexplored passage between North and Middle Dundas Islands. As it was, the set of the current was driving us fast to the northward, and we were finally, and with great reluctance, compelled to bear away for the passage between Zayas Island and the North Dundas. Easing off the sheets a little, we now ran before the troubled seas, and soon got into the smooth water under the lee of Dundas Island. At noon we crossed the head of Chatham Sound, and brought up, in ten fathoms, opposite the Fort in Port Simpson Harbour, at two, p.m. During all this time the barometer was rapidly going down; and shortly after making all snug, the gale increased in violence; terrific squalls, accompanied by sleet and rain, swept down the rising ground behind the Fort, causing the "Otter" to careen, and twisting her round like a feather. Our holding ground was good, however, and with forty fathoms of chain out, we took it coolly. Morrison soon came on board, when we "spliced the main brace," and wished success to the ill-fated "George Wright," then out, to the northward, on her last and disastrous voyage to Sitka. This unfortunate vessel must have foundered or gone ashore during this very gale, which had not yet attained its height. On the morning of the 5th, the barometer stood at 28·68 inches, and the storm still continued. By-and-by the wind veered by south and west, causing a rise in the mercury, and giving us hopes of a speedy cessation of bad weather. It was not, however, until the morning of the 6th that we again got up steam, and made a fresh attempt to continue our voyage.

At six, a.m., steam being up, we left Port Simpson; and running between Finlayson Island and the mainland, steamed down Chatham Sound, passing Metlah-Catlah at 9.15, and reaching Willa-Claugh at eleven o'clock, where we took on board some passengers and freight—among the former the Rev. M. Tomlinson, of the Naas, then on his way to Victoria. It had now calmed down, but the surrounding high land was completely enveloped in mist, which quite cut off the view of the Skeena, close to which we then were. Willa-Claugh consists of one or two wooden shanties, jammed up against a dark precipitous mountain, and presents a most forlorn appearance. It is situated on the north side of the North Skeena Passage, and about twenty miles from Port Essington. The land on every side is steep, and rises in places to a height of two or three thousand feet above the water, offering no level beaches, while the late rains, having completely washed away all traces of snow from the green timber, invested the dark mountains with a yet gloomier hue. Six or seven miles to the south-west lay the huge black mass of Porcher Island, which interposed its rugged wooded peaks between us and the ocean outside. Where we now lay, with forty fathoms of dark-blue water beneath us, the surface was as smooth as that of an inland lake, and the now placid waters of the Pacific kissed the dark frowning rocks at the base of Tree Point, without a murmur of dissent.

At two, p.m., having taken on board all our passengers and freight, including the clergyman and a fur-hunting Jew from Victoria, who was returning home with a few bales of deerskins and some fur seals, we steamed slowly down Arthur Channel, sighting the Ogden passage for a few minutes, and then shaped a mid-channel course down the Grenville Canal, a passage between the mainland and Pitt Island, fifty miles long, and from half-a-mile to a mile and a-half in width. On each side of this deep arm of the sea, the mountains rose, sometimes sheer to a height of two thousand feet, and, in some instances, reaching an altitude of nearly four thousand feet above the water; their dark sides shrouded in an almost palpable mist, which hung like a pall over them, and wet our decks like rain. About eleven, p.m. we passed the entrance to the Douglas Channel, at the upper end of which the Kitimat River enters the Pacific. The dawn of day met us as we began to feel the influence of the ocean swell rolling in through Milbank Sound, which we crossed by 8.40, a.m, and running down the Seaforth Channel, dropped anchor in the beautiful little harbour of Bellabella precisely at eleven o'clock. Here we took an ox on board, and after an interchange of commodities with the man in charge of the Hudson's Bay Company's post, were again under weigh at forty minutes past twelve, a.m., *en route* for Bella Coula, *via* the Gunboat Passage. Ten miles of very intricate navigation through a channel across which, in some places, one might have thrown a stone, brought us into Dean Channel, another deep inlet varying in width from three quarters of a mile to two miles, and walled in on either hand by huge mountains, the summits of which were lost to view in the dense mists above. On entering this fiord, we were met by a furious wind, which swept down through the Cascade Range with sufficient force to almost arrest our progress, but, as we had the advantage of smooth water, the "Otter" made headway, and at seven o'clock we rounded the north end of King Island, bringing up in twenty fathoms abreast of Bella Coula River at 9.45 p.m.

The Hudson Bay Company have here a small post, where a trifling trade is carried on with the Indians. The post of Bella Coula is situated at the furthest extremity of the Bentinck North Arm, and is about fifty-five miles from the south end of King's Island. It may be fairly said to lie within the Cascade Range of mountains, which tower above it on three sides. The level and low bottom on which the post is built extends far inland between high mountains, and through it flows the shallow little Bella Coula River, which is navigable for canoes a long distance up. In former years this was the route to the Frazer River, and pack animals were wont to perform the distance from the salt water to Alexandria in ten days. For some reason this route has been condemned, but from the accounts given by parties familiar with it, I should think there would be no great difficulty in constructing a road. As an eligible point for a railroad terminus, Bella Coula, however, labours under two serious disadvantages which are insuperably objectionable. During the early part of summer, the snows from the surrounding mountains flood the river, which sometimes overflows its banks, inundating the flat on either side to a depth of four or five feet. The second objection is that the anchorage is far from being good. Almost unfathomable depth of water, in the immediate proximity of a flat which dries in great part at low tide, renders the anchorage difficult and insecure. So sudden does the water deepen off this shoal, which is the result of the accumulated silt of ages, that a small vessel may have her anchor down in twenty-five or thirty fathoms, and still touch the mud-bank astern. Ours was a case in point, for, at low water, I could almost have jumped off the "Otter's" taffrail to the mud-bank below, while a stone's throw from the bow there were probably ninety fathoms. Another objection to the place is the limited amount of space, the flat not being over a mile in width. On the other hand a *sailing* ship might pass weeks at the entrance to Fitzhugh Sound, while waiting for a slant of favourable wind to run up; for to beat against the terrific force of the winter storms which blow up and down these narrow fiords, with almost irresistible violence, would be simply impossible.

We remained here for twenty-two hours, during which interval a quantity of firewood and some very inferior furs were shipped. At half-past seven o'clock on the evening of the 8th the anchor was again weighed, and we ran down the inlet, bound for Fort Rupert, the most northern of the Hudson Bay Company's forts on the Island of Vancouver. We had in tow a large canoe filled with a dirtier lot of Indians than even the filthy wretches of Kitwuncole. They were bound for some village down the coast, and Captain Lewis had kindly proffered them a tow rope as far as our respective routes coincided.

At 9.50 p.m. the north-east end of King Island was passed, and by three o'clock on the following morning its southern extremity had vanished in the mists astern. Shortly before breakfast we passed Safety Cove, and at ten o'clock, Cape Caution was distant six miles, and bore east by south. We now set all our available canvas, and "flattening" everything aft, shaped a course for Cape James, the north-eastern part of Hope Island. We were now crossing Queen Charlotte Sound, which fully maintained its reputation for bad weather, a stiff south-easter, laden with moisture, causing quite a heavy sea, and, in the case of some of the passengers, an unpleasant feeling in the epigastric region, as the cadaverous hue of their countenances betrayed. At noon, we threaded the intricate Shadwell Passage, where some years ago an American man-of-war was lost, and, at a quarter to one o'clock, were heading east-half-north down Goletas Channel, bringing up in Beaver Harbour, at 3.45 p.m., opposite, and within a cable length of Fort Rupert.

The climate and general appearance of the land had undergone a decided change since crossing Queen Charlotte Sound. With the rugged mountains of the mainland, we had left the snows and frosts of winter, and seemed now to be getting into another climate, as we gaily steamed down the beautiful waters which wash the eastern margin of Vancouver Island. The vast scale upon which nature has built up the repellent shores of the mainland, now left to the north, was changed for one less pretentious but of far more pleasing aspect. The narrow passage between Hope and Galiano Islands had the appearance of the beautiful scenery of the Thousand Islands of the St. Lawrence, while the shores of Vancouver, which we now had on our starboard hand, although rocky, wore an agreeable aspect, and contrasted most favourably with the recollections of the gloomy scenes through which we had lately passed. Not a particle of snow was now to be seen, and the air had a balmy feeling very exhilirating to the spirits.

After delivering some cargo, and receiving the returns of Fort Rupert, we continued on, stopping for a few minutes in Alert Bay, where we picked up a passenger. The weather had now become rather moist, and towards the morning a steady rain set in. We kept on, however, in spite of the darkness, entering Johnston's Straits at ten, p.m. This arm of the sea has a width of from three-quarters of a mile to a mile and a-half, and on the Vancouver Island side there are some high mountain ranges which rise to an altitude of four and five thousand feet. At 8 a.m., on the morning of the 10th, we entered Discovery Passage, passing through the Seymour Narrows at half-past nine. When running through this, the narrowest passage between Vancouver Island and the numerous islands which lie between it and the mainland of British Columbia, we had the advantage of perfectly smooth water, the tide being on the turn, and there being little or no wind ; but there are times, especially when tide and wind oppose each other, when a very heavy sea renders boating dangerous. The distance between Maud Island on the east and Wilfred Point on the Vancouver side of the Narrows, is little more than four cable lengths, and the reader may imagine with what force the tides rush through this contracted space. About two and a-half cable lengths from Maud Island, or say two-thirds of the way across, there is a sunken rock called " The Ripple," which has three fathoms and a-half of water over it at low tide. It is across this narrow strait that the railroad from the mainland *must* be taken, if the destiny of Vancouver Island be ever joined continuously with that of the continental portion of the Dominion. In the event of the Alberni Canal (to which access is had through Barclay Sound on the west coast of the island) being chosen for the terminus of the road—a very unlikely selection—a line about eighty miles in length would be required from the Seymour Narrows to that point. But as Victoria will, in all probability, be the terminal point on the Pacific, there will be needed about one hundred and sixty miles of railway in order to connect that rising little town with the great bridge at the Narrows—for a great and serious undertaking it will be to build a bridge sufficiently strong to answer the purpose, on account of the depth of water, and the strong tides which rush up and down at a rate ranging from five to eight knots per hour. Eight hundred and seventy-five yards of such rapid water, in depth from ten to forty fathoms, with, in all that distance, but one resting place, twenty-one feet below the surface at low water, will be no slight difficulty to overcome. The distance between the Seymour Narrows and the mainland, on the western shore of Bute Inlet, is probably twenty-five miles, and between those points several bridges will be needed to connect them, thence, by following the steep and rocky shores of the Bute Inlet for a distance of about fifty miles, the mouth of the Homalco River, situated at the head of the inlet, will be reached. From this very imperfect description of that portion of the Canada Pacific Road, included between the mouth of the Homalco River, and the shores of Vancouver Island, a distance of, say seventy-five miles, the reader may infer that the expense of road construction will be very great, perhaps greater than the advantages to be derived from the immediate connection with Vancouver Island might warrant; however, the gentlemen who represent Vancouver Island in the Parliament of the Dominion, will be enabled to do their "mileage" without breaks, and with a certain amount of comfort, which is an advantage not to be overlooked.

At ten o'clock we met the full force of the flood

tide, which, aided by a rather strong south-east breeze suddenly sprung up, considerably retarded our progress. At one o'clock we were abreast of Cape Mudge, eleven miles below the Narrows; but the captain, finding we could make nothing of it, decided to run back to the shelter of Duncan Bay, where we remained until two o'clock the following morning. We then got under weigh, and steamed to Comox, dropping our anchor in Port Augusta at seven a.m.

This is a beautiful harbour, and the gently rising ground near the beach looked very inviting, lighted up, as it was, by the bright February sun, which gilded the snowy summits of the Beaufort range of mountains, distant ten miles. The weather was also perfectly delightful, the morning being like those we have on the Ottawa towards the close of April. At seven, a.m., the thermometer stood at 48 deg. in the shade; and the change from the almost Arctic appearance of the coast north of Queen Charlotte Sound, to the smiling, spring-like landscape now seen from the "Otter's" deck, was difficult to realize. After taking in some freight, on account of the Hudson's Bay Company, we weighed once more for Nanaimo, the Newcastle of Vancouver Island; at ten, a.m., passing through Bayne's Sound, and keeping Denman's Island on the port hand. When a few miles past the latter, we sighted Mount Baker (height 10,700 feet), which bore about due east magnetic, and was then distant one hundred and twenty geographical miles. Off Qualicum River we began to feel the influence of the balmy western breeze from the Pacific, which enabled us to make sail. This was one of the most delightful afternoons imaginable. The Canadian reader will be, doubtless, surprised when I say that we lolled away an hour or two upon the "Otter's" deck (this was the 11th February), basking in the bright sun, and fanned by the most delicious of breezes. It was like running down the trades, and brought back recollections of former voyages in the sunny seas of the southern hemisphere. The appearance of the land, within three miles of which we were now running, was very pretty, and devoid of ruggedness.

CHAPTER XII.

GEOLOGY OF VANCOUVER ISLAND.

JUST AS the sun was sinking behind the hills, in the rear of Nanaimo, we entered that harbour, and, for the first time during the voyage, ranged up alongside a substantial wharf, and immediately under the Coal Company's derrick. The "Sir James Douglas" was here, and a large American barque lay beneath a coal "shoot," taking in a cargo of that valuable commodity for San Francisco. The Coal Company delivers the mineral for $5 and $5.50 per ton; and, I believe, it sells in the San Francisco market at $12—thus leaving a large margin of profit to the carriers.

Vancouver Island has large deposits of excellent coal, which is found in many places from Fort Rupert down to Nanaimo, which will doubtless, ere long, prove a source of great wealth to the island. As a minute description of the geological character of Vancouver Island may be read with interest, I give an extract from Dr. Hector's Report upon that subject. Speaking of his visit to Nanaimo, the Doctor says:—

"At this place, coal has been worked by the Hudson Bay Company since 1854, and the total output up to January, 1860, has been about twelve thousand tons. Through the kindness of Mr. Nichol, the gentleman in charge of the works, and Mr. Pearce, of the Land Office, I am able to show a plan of the workings, and also a map of the neighbourhood, in which I have inserted my own observations of the geology. At the time of my visit there were three pits in operation, giving employment to thirty miners and a number of labourers. The former are principally Scotch and Staffordshire men, who have been brought out to the country at the Hudson's Bay Company's expense; but the greater number of the latter are Indians, small tribes of whom come and settle at the mines, and work for a short time, till they tire of the uncongenial life, when they leave, to make room for another band. The irregular supply of labour, from this cause, adds greatly to the uncertainty and expense of the workings. When working in the best seams at Nanaimo, a miner can put out two and a-half tons per day. The shipment from Nanaimo in the month of January, 1860, was two thousand tons, the trade having at that time been suddenly extended by the demand consequent upon the establishment of gas-works at Portland,

Oregon, and several other places. This extension of the market was supplied from a large stock that was lying on hand at the time; but, from having been exposed to the action of the weather for many years, it was of very inferior quality. In spite of this, however, I understand that the demand has continued steady throughout last year, and that the coal has been much used in California for making gas, instead of that brought from the Eastern States, as heretofore.

"Coal from the same description of strata has been also worked to some degree on the opposite side of the Gulf of Georgia, at Billingham Bay, and also at Cooze Bay, in Washington territory. Although it has been found in many other localities along the coast, as I shall mention, after describing the formation, these are the only places where it has been worked to some extent. The whole formation associated with the lignite or coal beds is very extensively developed along the Pacific coast, and has generally been considered as of tertiary age, excepting from the first accounts sent home, which, as there were no fossils, induced geologists to consider them as carboniferous. Some fossils transmitted to the Jermyn street Museum, many years ago, were first rightly recognized by the late Professor E. Forbes as being cretaceous; but the localities were undescribed, and, in the absence of sections, it was impossible to deduce anything from them regarding the age of the coal beds.

"The observations I have now to offer respecting these strata will, I believe, put their age beyond doubt as cretaceous; but rightly to understand the value to be attached to them requires me to give, first, a sketch of the physical features of the district.

"The southern part of Vancouver Island, where the town of Victoria is built, is composed of metamorphic rocks, with occasional beds of crystalline limestone. This district, and also the central portion of the island, is, as may be expected from the formation, everywhere hilly, and even mountainous, with only limited patches of fertile soil in the valleys. However, the scanty soil on the rocky hills supports a fine growth of timber, so that they are almost invariably wooded to their summits. In the immediate neighbourhood of Victoria there is, nevertheless, a good deal of fine open land, dotted with small oak trees. On passing to the north, through the Canal de Nuro, the islands of the archipelago, between Vancouver Island and the mainland, are composed of strata of sandstone and conglomerate, which form lofty cliffs, overhanging intricate but beautiful inlets. The junction between these two formations was not observed; but I think it is south of San Juan Island, and from thence across to Vancouver Island by Sandwich Point, and thence northwards a little way back from the coast, leaving a narrow slip of fine land.

"These sandstone and conglomerate strata have a uniform strike of from N.N.W. and S.S.E., and in passing along the shore of Saluma Island they were observed to form several well-marked synclinal troughs, till, on passing through the Plumper Pass, they dip gently to the N.E., under the waters of the Gulf of Georgia. Section No. 1 (on the map) merely shows the plications of the strata as observed on passing along the shore once in a canoe, and again in a steamer,—the nature of the beds not being ascertained beyond the general fact that they are thick-bedded sandstone and conglomerates, with sometimes strata of clay shale. The sandstones are much acted on by the weather, and at the water-line the sea has generally worn in them caves and hollows. The conglomerates form the highest beds of the series, and are of immense thickness.

"After passing the Plumper Pass, in proceeding north through Trincomalee Channel, Galiano Island, to the west, presents cliffs about eight hundred feet high of the sandstone and conglomerate strata, with a gentle dip to the east; sometimes spits or low promontories of the strata run parallel with the coast, enclosing narrow bays. The west side of the channel, on Salt Spring Island, is a low shelving coast, heavily timbered to the water's edge, and exposing outcrops of grey and blue clay shales, which dip to the east. The portion of this island which is occupied by these shales is the finest land for settlement I have seen on the coast ; but the southern part is mountainous, rising to the height of 2,300 feet. It is on the north part of Salt Spring Island that the saline springs are situated, from which it gets its name. They seem to escape from the shales, and occur in spots clear from timber, and covered with green moist vegetation, abounding in saliferous plants. Round the orifices from which the brine escapes there have formed conical mounds of granuar calcareous scinter, stained with iron ; but in summer there is said to be an abundant deposit of pure white salt.

" North of Salt Spring Island the strata preserve the same strike and general appearance all the way to Nanaimo, the island forming long spits of sandstone and conglomerate, with precipitous shores to the west. Just below the rapids the shales were again noticed resting on the sandstone, and both dipping to the west. At very low tide a thick seam of lignite is exposed at this point and on the island opposite, and to the east I found a thin seam in the sandstones at Nanaimo. The sandstone country occupies a broader belt along the shore of Vancouver Island than further to the south, but immediately to the north the strike changes to nearly east and west on Newcastle Island, and on Fossil Point the lowest beds were seen to rest on igneous rocks, which continued to occupy the coast for the few miles I went further to the north. At the head of the Gulf of Georgia the sandstones are again said to form the islands that crowd the narrow channel which separates Vancouver Island from the mainland, and also a great extent of both shores. From Comox to Valdez Inlet, which is situated in this locality, some of the fossils I have were procured by Mr. McKay of the Hudson Bay Company. Also at the extreme north of the island, at Fort Rupert, Mr. Lord, of the Boundary Commission, observed the sandstones and thick beds of lignite dipping out to sea.

"At many points along the eastern shore of the Gulf of Georgia these strata have been detected with the associated lignite beds. North of Howse Sound the mountains closely hug the sea coast, but south of that they retire along the north shore of Burrard's Inlet to the S.E., so as to be sixty miles inland at where the boundary meets them, thus leaving a very heavily timbered tract, which forms the only level country in British Columbia east of the Cascade range. Most of this district is covered by shingle terraces and other superficial deposits which obscure the underlying strata, but at Burrard's Inlet, eight miles north of the entrance to Fraser River, lignite and sandstones containing fossil leaves have been sent home by H.M.S. "Plumper." Also on Fraser River, near Fort Langley, and on its tributary, Pitt River, the lignite has been observed, and again at

Bellingham Bay, south of the boundary line, so that it is probable that they underlie the greater part of the region.

"Three hundred yards from the shore, in the channel that passes between Newcastle Island and the Fossil Point, is a row of islands composed of very fine conglomerate, that might be termed "gravel stone," in beds that dip to the S.S.E. at fifteen degrees, these beds contain small fragments of carbonized wood.

"A quarter of a mile further on, in the direction of the dip, on the north end of Newcastle Island, there are high cliffs of sandstone which preserve the same direction. They seem to be rather more disturbed than the strata that form the islands in the channel, but this appearance is exaggerated by the great amount of false bedding. The strata of sandstone continue to preserve the same direction of dip all along the coast of Newcastle Island, but gradually becoming more horizontal towards the southern extremity. At Exit Channel occur the seams of coal, the lowest of which has been worked to a considerable extent, while the existence of the other has only been found by boring. The outcrop of these two seams has been ascertained on the east shore of the island, where they have the same character and relative position, thus showing that they are continuous to that extent. The lowest bed of lignite is called the Newcastle seam, and is worked by levels.

driven into the outcrop as it rises with the high bank from the shore. The coal or lignite is six feet thick, with a floor of sandstone, and the roof of a very tough conglomerate of very small pebbles. The strata have a dip of twenty degrees, so that the method employed succeeds well for taking out small quantities.

"This mine was not being worked when I visited it, but there were large heaps of the coal waiting for a market, that had been lying there for some years, so that I could judge the effect of the weather on it with great facility. The surface was turned to a rusty brown, and the masses showed a tendency to break up with a slaty fracture; otherwise the exposure had worked but little change.

"Along the shore of the island, to the south, the strata of argillaceous sandstone are seen to dip steadily in the same direction, but with less and less inclination, till at the southern extremity they are almost horizontal. On Douglas Island there is said to be another seam of coal from the shale along with which the fossil leaves are generally procured. I had not an opportunity of visiting it, however, myself. On the coast of Nanaimo Harbour, the strike of the strata is quite different, but yet they preserve the same character and sequence, Exit Channel seeming to mark a great fault. The little peninsula on which the Hudson Bay Company's establishment stands, and where the coal was first discovered, is also another dislocated portion of the strata, as may be seen by reference to the map.

"At Nanaimo, as on Newcastle Island, there are two seams, the "Newcastle" and the "Douglas," the first of which is everywhere about six feet in thickness, with sometimes a floor of fire-clay, but more generally of sandstone, and the roof consisting of the fine conglomerate bed, about sixty feet thick, on which rests the Douglas seam, with an average thickness of from three and a-half to four feet. The roof of this seam is sometimes of iron-clay shale, but more often of the same tough conglomerate that it rests upon. On Chase River, one and a-quarter miles to the south, the outcrop of a seam has been discovered and worked to a small extent, which they consider to be the Newcastle seam, and as it occurs right in the line of strike, and they have ascertained the outcrop at several points, it is probable that the beds of coal are continuous thus far at least.

"In the mines they have met several 'stone faults,' where the floor rises up and throws the coal seam out for several fathoms. It is generally represented, however, by a carbonaceous parting. These faults are a source of great expense in the working, as the conglomerate to be pierced is exceedingly tough and compact, so that the blast only brings it away in small pieces. The extent or character of the workings can be ascertained better from an inspection of the map, however, than by any description.

" In proceeding along the coast towards the mouth of Nanaimo River, the strata consists of argillaceous sandstones, with a similar character to those of the southern part of Newcastle Island, and preserving a steady though gentle dip to the E. by S. A short way above the entrance to the river, in the sandstones, there is a thin seam of coal, the position of which was pointed out to me by Mr. Nichol, as the river was too high to allow us to see it. Continuing to ascend the river, which is of small size, we found low exposures of the sandstone, still with the dip to the E., and at Fossil Bank, three or four miles from the mouth, they are overlaid conformably by dark purple clays, filled with septaria, which yield cretaceous fossils. The dip of the beds is ten degrees to the E. by N., and the clay strata were clearly seen to rest on the hard-bedded sandstones. I found inoceramus, baculites and some other fragments of fossils, of which other specimens are also among those obtained by Mr. Bauerman at this place. I was told at Nanaimo that ammonites have frequently been found there of large size, and from Mr. McKay I obtained a number of fossils, some of which he collected in this locality; but others, having the same appearance, and also contained in septaria, he procured from Comux and Valdez Inlet, at the head of the Gulf of Georgia; but these two sets of specimens have been unfortunately mixed together. For a couple of miles the Nanaimo River flows through these clay strata, and then turns again from the S.W., and in ascending the sandstone strata were again found to recur, as in the lower part of the river, but with a more rapid dip. At the Canon these sandstones form precipices about one hundred feet in height, forming a narrow gorge six hundred yards long, through which the river flows. The beds dip at fifteen degrees to the E.N.E., and are very like those of Newcastle Island.

"From under these sandstones in ascending the river, hard beds of the gravel conglomerate cropped out with great regularity, separated by soft beds of red and greenish clay. These probably correspond to the group with the lignite. at Nanaimo, but I failed in finding any trace of it beyond fragments of carbonized wood. The strata from the fossil bank up to the river, as far as I went, are shown in section 3.

"The total thickness of the beds from the lignite to the clays at Fossil Bank, I estimated at six hundred to seven hundred feet, but I had no opportunity of making any exact measurement. Between Nanaimo River on the coast there is a tract of very fine country, and it is probably occupied by the septaria clays, which, as I mentioned before, are seen a little south of the rapid.

"At Bellingham Bay, the sections given on the map

were taken by Mr. Pemberton, and show that the lignite occurs in large quantity at that place. Lieutenant Trowbridge, in describing the strata there, says they are two thousand feet thick, and including in all one hundred and ten feet of the lignite coal. His sections are probably, however, all of the same group of strata, being at different points in the strike, which gives rise to the apparently enormous thickness.

"The analysis of the coal from Bellingham Bay, which is generally considered inferior to that of Nanaimo, is given in the Pacific Railway Report, as follows:

$$\begin{aligned} &\text{Carbon} \ldots \ldots 47\cdot 63 \\ &\text{Bitumen} \ldots \ldots 50\cdot 22 \\ &\text{Ash} \ldots \ldots 2\cdot 15 \end{aligned}$$

"This coal has been sold in San Francisco at \$18 to \$22 per ton (75s. to 91s. 6d. sterling).

"Lignite coal has also been worked for the same market from Coon Bay, which has the following composition:

$$\begin{aligned} &\text{Carbon} \ldots \ldots 46\cdot 54 \\ &\text{Gaseous matter} \ldots \ldots 50\cdot 27 \\ &\text{Ash} \ldots \ldots 3\cdot 19 \end{aligned}$$

"Conrad states that shells from this locality are of Miocene age. At Binicia, above San Francisco, coal also occurs, and was wrought for some time, but the dip was too steep.

"In Newbury's report on the geology of this part of California, I have not seen any notice of where Binicia lignite occurs in his sections; but between Binicia and the sea, he describes three thousand feet of strata, the lowest beds being of sandstone and shales, resting on and penetrated by serpentine and trap (the same which are so highly charged with ores of copper and mercury further to the south). These are followed by green and brown shales, coarse, soft sandstone, fine sandstone and shales, with pecten, natica, mactra, and filaria, and these conglomerates and tufas, the whole lying at an angle of thirty degrees. Towards Binicia are thin-bedded clays, with shark's teeth. Up Feather River, a tributary of the Sacramento River at Chico Creek, a calciferous sandstone is described containing nucula, mactra, and other tertiary forms, but from the same place are baculites, inacerami, and ammonites, which Meek considers as proving the existence of upper cretaceous strata at that place; so that it is probable that there are strata of both ages, but included in the same disturbances, and it is not unlikely that the section from Binicia to the sea may also include cretaceous strata.

"The existence of coal or lignite on the Pacific coast, of quality fit for the purposes of raising steam, is of great commercial importance, and that obtained from Nanaimo is as yet admitted to be the best in the market.

"If these beds are, therefore, discovered to be persistent, so that they can be worked to advantage on a large scale, there is little doubt that this coal, even though it be an imperfect substitute for the finer coal we are accustomed to in this country, will form a valuable source of wealth to the new British colony. Already it is extensively used by the British navy on that station, and it was found to require only a slight modification in the method of feeding the fires to make it highly effective as a steam generator.

"As beds of coal of similar quality exist in the Islands of Japan and Formosa, we would thus have the supply of fuel at the extremity of the line of the great sea voyage, if the route from England by the Canadas, Saskatchewan, and British Columbia, to China, and the east, were adopted, a natural fitness not to be overlooked in considering such a scheme."

CHAPTER XIII.

NANAIMO TO SAN FRANCISCO.

Nanaimo—San Juan—The Boundary Dispute—Victoria—Esquimault—Olympia—Opposition Stages—A Humiliating Breakdown—Washington Territory—A Model Hotel—Reach Portland—On board the "Oriflamme"—Astoria—Arrival at San Francisco.

THE little town of Nanaimo has increased since the Doctor's visit. The pits, and all the appliances for the extraction and shipment of coal, are on a true English scale, and extremely creditable to the enterprising firm which conducts the business. There is a substantial iron tram-road, about half-a-mile long, by which the coal is rapidly and economically transferred from the pit's mouth to the wharf, where, by a special contrivance, similar to that used in English ports, it is dumped into the ship's hold.

On the morning of the 12th, Mr. Green, the purser, and I paid a visit to the pit, and were preparing to descend, when a warning whistle caused us to return to the "Otter," which had just finished coaling. We had barely jumped on board when the lines were cast off; and leaving the wharf, we steamed through the Dodd Narrows, and down Trincomalee Channel, between Admiral and Pender Islands, and into the Swanson Channel. In the afternoon we passed the picturesque island of San Juan, which, had the late arbitration decided fairly, would now belong to Vancouver Island, instead of being the property of our jealous neighbours. The Haro Straits, between six and seven miles wide, which separate San Juan from Vancouver Island, could be effectually commanded from San Juan by heavy ordnance; and the passage of ships from the Pacific to Bute Inlet might be seriously interfered with in the event of hostilities between Canada and the States. At five, p.m., after rounding Discovery and Trial Islands, we entered the intricate channel leading into the harbour of Victoria, and ranged up alongside the Hudson's Bay Company's wharf at six, p.m.—thus completing another stage of the long journey from Fort Garry.

As Victoria has been described already by various writers, it is sufficient for me to say that it is a little town of five or six thousand inhabitants, was originally located by the Hudson's Bay Company, possesses a small harbour, can boast of gas, has a theatre, any number of saloons, and one or two fair hotels, of which the Driard House is the best. A short distance to the westward of Victoria lies the commodious harbour of Esquimault, where vessels of large tonnage can always anchor.

Finding that the steamer "Prince Alfred" had just left for San Francisco, I determined to proceed to California by the way of Puget Sound and Portland, in the State of Oregon. On the morning of the 18th February, I accordingly took passage on board the American steamer "North Pacific," which leaves Victoria twice a-week for Olympia, a little town situated at the very extreme end of the Sound, and distant by water from Victoria about one hundred and twenty nautical miles. The day was beautiful, but a stiffish north-east breeze coming from the snowy Cascades, rendered an overcoat necessary. This vessel was built after the fashion of American river steamers, and had the usual tier of high cabins, and a spacious saloon, which was well filled with passengers. In two hours and a-half we crossed the strait, and, rounding Point Wilson, turned into Port Townsend, distant thirty-five miles from Victoria. Some of our passengers disembarked at this little village; and, after a few minutes' delay, we pushed on, touching at some intermediate points, and reached Olympia at two, a.m. on the 19th. A considerable lumber business is carried on in the little settlements bordering on the Sound, and, at nearly all the ports we touched, vessels of large size were loading sawn lumber for San Francisco and South American ports. Several large barques passed us outward bound for Valparaiso and San Francisco, which seem to be the principal markets for the Puget Sound lumber.

In the morning, those of our passengers who, like myself, were *en route* for Portland, went ashore, and breakfasted at a restaurant in the principal street of the town, before taking the stage for Tenino, fifteen miles distant, and the most western point which the Northern Pacific road has reached. Having, while on board the " Northern Pacific," secured a through ticket for Portland, for the sum of $13.50 (gold), I proceeded, after breakfast, to the stage office, and depositing my valise in the care of the stage-driver, started on foot, giving that functionary to understand that he would overtake me on the road.

Olympia claims, I believe, to be the capital of Washington Territory, and has the appearance of having reached its present estate with too rapid strides. Its principal revenue appears to be derived from the stir and business created by the passenger traffic between Portland and Victoria. There are several very fair shops, and the place has the neat and trim appearance which Americans generally succeed so well in giving to their towns. Following the main street for half-a-mile, the road ascends a pretty steep hill, and enters an extensive pine forest. The soil is very light and sandy, offering but small inducement to farmers. Indeed, the chief trade of this territory appears to be lumber, which is divided into two branches, viz., the milling business, carried on separately; while that of procuring logs is conducted by men who devote their attention to them alone, and usually get them out by contract with the millers. A couple of miles beyond Olympia, the road crossed a small inlet, where some extensive mills were in full operation. Beyond this I passed through a moderately level and partially burnt country, diversified by occasional open tracts, where now and again a settler's home could be seen.

Six miles on, a waggon laden with "Celestials," and bearing upon its white canvas covering, in gigantic letters, the words, "Opposition Stage," passed me, and, immediately after, the legitimate conveyance, drawn by two horses, came up. The driver, reining up, desired me to get in as quickly as possible, as he wished to get past "the darned opposition cuss." The occupants of the vehicle in which I now found myself seated were, an Oregon cattle-owner, reputed very wealthy, a California gentleman on his way home to San Francisco, and last, though not least, the ex-Governor of Washington Territory. We bumped along at a fair speed, overtaking and passing the "opposition," to the driver of which the Oregon man maliciously offered a tow-rope. We had hardly made a couple of hundred yards past that vehicle, when the tire of our hind wheel snapped, and almost immediately after, the wheel itself became so ricketty that we were obliged to stop, the "opposition" driver passing us, and sarcastically volunteering to detain the train at Tenino until we came up. We had now no alternative but to proceed on foot, so, each man shouldering as many of his personal effects as he could conveniently carry, we plodded on through the dense pine woods, and reached Tenino at half-past one. The conductor very obligingly detained the train for fifteen minutes, until we swallowed a hasty dinner, for which the moderate sum of fifty cents was charged.

Tenino was merely a temporary city, and consisted of the unfinished station and buildings of the Northern Pacific Road, now brought to this point from Kalama, another town of railway growth situated sixty miles to the southward, and on the right bank of the Columbia River. At this time the terminal point of the road was still kept secret, but the general opinion pointed either to Bellingham Bay, situated one hundred and sixty miles to the northward, or to Sinahomis, a harbour on Possession Sound. Although a daily train was run upon this road, the time allowed to reach Kalama was five hours, on account of the unfinished state of the permanent way. The road was not ballasted, and extreme caution was necessary in some places. The country through which this piece of road passes was heavily timbered, and for the greater distance passably level; some rather shaky trestle bridges were also crossed.

Throughout, the soil was wretched, being generally of a sandy or gravelly character; altogether, Washington Territory has not much to boast of, excepting its pine and coal, the latter being much inferior to that of Vancouver Island. Between Tenino and the Columbia River, the country passed through was sparsely settled, and inferior in every respect to what I had expected from the glowing accounts given of it by the partisans of the Northern Pacific Road. Before reaching Kalama, the railroad follows the low banks of the Columbia River for several miles, over alluvial flats, which appear to flood during high-water. Kalama is a town of some two years' growth, and possesses a large and handsome hotel, situated high up on the steep hill, on the side of which the town is built. The Kazano House was a model of cleanliness, and a really sumptuous repast was served up in the most approved modern style by Chinese waiters. This house is built entirely of wood, but is of great size, and fitted up in as comfortable a manner as could be desired.

The next morning, at five, a.m., the passengers for Portland, myself among the number, embarked on a very comfortable stern-wheel steamer, and ascending the Columbia River, reached Portland on the Willamette, at half-past nine. Proceeding at once to the Oregon Steam-ship Company's office, I secured a berth on board the side-wheel steamer "Oriflamme," advertised to leave for San Francisco, on the following day at four p.m. For this I paid $30 in gold, and proceeding with Mr. S——, of San Francisco, to the St. Charles Hotel, we put up in that large and commodious establishment.

Portland, the capital of Oregon, is situated upon the left bank of the Willamette, and about one hundred miles from the mouth of the Columbia River, which is joined by the former a few miles below the city. It is handsomely and regularly built, and has some good streets and very fine buildings. The population is about ten thousand. Among the public buildings worthy of notice is the market-house, which, for neatness and cleanliness, far surpasses similar institutions I have seen in the largest cities in Canada. A considerable trade in lumber, grain and cattle is carried on here, and ships of large tonnage load alongside the well-constructed wharves. On the opposite side of the Willamette, the terminus of the Oregon Central Railroad is situated. This line follows the right bank of the river for a considerable way, and is intended to connect with the California and Oregon Road. It is already constructed as far as Eugene City, some one hundred and twenty miles to the southward. On the Portland side, a branch of the same line is projected to Astoria, at the mouth of the Columbia River.

On the 21st February, at four, p.m., the "Oriflamme" cast off from the wharf, after having embarked about one hundred and twenty passengers for San Francisco. We reached Astoria the next morning at ten, a.m., and took on board a pilot for there is a dangerous bar which, about seven miles below the town, obstructs the entrance of the Columbia River.

Astoria is a dead-and-alive kind of place, and, by all accounts, is retrograding. The Columbia is about five miles wide opposite here, and several ships were lying just inside the bar, waiting for a slant of favourable wind to run out. At half-past ten we cast off, and steamed for the bar, which was fortunately now quite smooth, the weather having been settled for the last few days. The channel is not very wide, but as its direction is first westward, and then suddenly changes to W.S.W., sailing ships often require to wait some time for a suitable wind to cross. During the prevalence of south-west gales, a heavy sea sets in, which breaks completely across the channel, and renders the entrance to the Columbia River extremely dangerous. Many ships have been lost here, and the place is consequently much dreaded by mariners. We were fairly outside at noon, when the square foresail and topsail were set, and we were now on our way down the coast for San Francisco. On the 23rd, at ten, a.m., we passed Cape Blanco, then ten miles distant. The weather was fine, with a light breeze from the northward, and we passed the "Prince Alfred," bound to

Victoria. At noon, to-day, the wind freshened, and by four, p.m., it was blowing a brisk gale, with a rather heavy sea running. Passed Cape Mendocino at eleven p.m. The weather the following day was perfectly delightful, with a nice breeze from the north. We entered the Golden Gate at eight, p.m., and reached the quay at San Francisco in an hour and a-half, the voyage from Portland having occupied seventy-seven hours and a-half, of which four were lost by detention from fog while in the Columbia River. On landing, I put up at the Grand Hotel, and left Oakland, *en route* for Ottawa, on the 26th February, reaching the capital of the Dominion eight days later, the round trip having occupied seven months and a few days.

CHAPTER XIV.

THE CANADA PACIFIC ROUTE.

MY NARRATIVE closes with a few remarks upon the great question of the day—one seriously involving the future prospects and interests of the Dominion—namely, that of the Canada Pacific Railway: its route westward from Fort Garry, its passage of the Rocky Mountains, and its most eligible terminal point upon the Pacific Coast.

The decision as to the rightful proprietorship of the Island of San Juan, lately made by the Emperor of Germany and his colleagues in the arbitration, will probably assist materially in forming a correct judgment as to the proper terminal point on the Pacific waters for the Interoceanic highway. Previous to the promulgation of the "fiat," the petty interests of New Westminster and Burrard's Inlet were, perhaps, suffered to influence, or, at any rate, to suspend judgment in this most important matter. The denizens of the Fraser River Valley sought, by every means in their power, to divert the course of the railroad to New Westminster. The sea-girt dwellers of Victoria blustered, and endeavoured to show up, in the most glowing colours, the advantages derivable from the selection of Esquimault as the railroad port; and, between the two, the Dominion Government had, doubtless, sore trouble. Now, however, the destinies of San Juan being no longer a matter for speculation, the petty and selfish interests of individuals will be disregarded, and the wise legislation of the Great Dominion, drawing much good out of a trifling evil, will, doubtless, sacrifice small and local interests to the general welfare, and choose the Bute Inlet for a terminus, until the great work of binding together the mainland with Vancouver Island shall be accomplished, when Esquimault, which is considered by naval authorities —the best in such matters—the safest and most accessible harbour north of San Francisco, will be at last uninterruptedly connected with the interior and eastern portions of the Continent.

Besides Esquimault and Burrard's Inlet, several other points have been brought forward as eligible for termini. A brief description of those places will, therefore, not be out of place.

The head of the Alberni Canal, situated up Barclay Sound, on the west coast of Vancouver Island, has been suggested. The promoters of such a scheme were, doubtless, ignorant of the dangers of the iron-girt western shores of Vancouver, and of Barclay

Sound in particular. So much do sea-faring men, not only officers of the Royal Navy, but old and experienced hands in the coast trade, understand and appreciate the dangers of this horrible coast, that, without one exception, all those to whom I have spoken or written upon the subject, emphatically denounce the choice of such a locality. Right across the principal entrance to Barclay Sound, and at intervals of one mile and a-half, stretch three clusters of sunken rocks, over which, in heavy weather, the deep sea of the Pacific breaks with a sullen roar; but during the terrific gales which sometimes rage from the north-west or south-west, the whole distance across, from Cape Beale to Storm Island (about seven nautical miles), and within which those sunken dangers occur, is a seething mass of troubled waters, among which the rocks referred to could be with very great difficulty distinguished. From twenty to fifty fathoms are found across the entrance; but the "fetch" of the Pacific is here so great, that whether or not buoys or beacons, if placed, would remain for any length of time in their positions, is problematical. The whole coast is here iron-bound, every point and headland of the Sound having to bear the brunt of the terrific swells which roll in upon their rocky and perpendicular sides with a violence unparalleled in any other part of the globe; and the slightest error in reckoning, which a stranger, entering for the first time, could not easily avoid, would inevitably result in immediate and total destruction.

Bella Coula, situated up the Bentinck North Arm, has also been spoken of; but to it I have already referred in my journey down the coast. As for the rivers Skeena and Naas, the geographical positions they occupy, apart from the consideration that to reach them from the east a railroad line would require to be carried, in a great measure, over some of the most unproductive and barren portions of Northern British Columbia, is sufficient to place them beyond further consideration.

From what I have seen of the coast of British Columbia, Bute Inlet, owing to its accessibility from the interior by the Chilcotin Valley, and from the fact of Vancouver Island being within practicable distance, appears to be the most suitable point on the mainland where the Canada Pacific Railway should debouch. Premising, then, that Bute Inlet will be chosen for a terminal point, we shall now consider the problem of how to reach it from Winnepeg, the capital of Manitoba, distant, in round numbers, sixteen hundred miles.

In the Canada Pacific Railroad Report of 1872, the route projected from Fort Garry westward, *via* Thunder Hill, the elbow of the North Saskatchewan, and the open plain country south of the North Saskatchewan, spanning the latter near the White Mud River, and thence to Lac Brulé, Jasper House, and the Tête Jaune Cache, does not pass over the best and most available land for settlement. Again, the difficulty of reaching Bute Inlet from the Tête Jaune Cache appears to be very great. The extreme roughness of the country between the Cache and Quesnel, either by Lac la Hache or the North Fork of the Fraser, would seem to bar progress by either route. However, it is within the bounds of possibility that a practicable route may be found; but even were such a route discovered, I emphatically maintain that the portion of the road between Thunder Hill and Jasper House, is not well chosen, with a view to successful settlement, and the economic construction and future maintenance of a railroad.

If the Dominion Government desire to construct a road which will open up the best land in the North-West, and if it be their wish to maintain it with economy, and little trouble from the *great snow difficulty without* and *within* the mountains, a question almost entirely obviated by the Peace River country route (for I venture to assert that the greatest depth of snow to be encountered, either on the south branch of the Peace, or near McLeod Lake, will not be anything like the deep snow met with on the Lower St. Lawrence, through which the Grand Trunk now passes), they must push the line through the country indicated in the following article published by me in the Ottawa *Citizen* of 24th October last:—

"At the present juncture, when the so-called Canada Pacific Railway scandal is occupying the attention of legislators and the public generally, it may not be amiss to offer some remarks upon the route or routes available for the very important highway destined not only to bring the remote shores of the Dominion within easy reach of each other, but also to open up the vast and now unoccupied lands of the North-West.

"That the route across the Rocky Mountains, *via* the Tête Jaune Cache, will be finally adopted, or, if chosen, that it will fulfil the conditions requisite, in order to meet the emergency of the case, is *not* the general belief. Against the selection of that route, there appear to be two rather powerful arguments. First, the difficulty of reaching the Bute Inlet from the Tête Jaune Cache; and secondly, the unsuitability of the section of country east of the Rocky Mountains crossed by that line for settlement.

"In order to reach this momentous question without circumlocution, we shall at once enter into a comparison between the route projected *via* the Tête Jaune Cache pass and one proposed by the writer, by way of Lac la Biche and the Peace River, crossing the Rocky Mountain range either by a supposed practicable and low pass, situated in about latitude $55\frac{1}{2}$ deg. N., or through the comparatively low gap in the Rocky Mountains by which the great Peace River finds its way from the British Columbian slopes at an elevation of about one thousand six hundred feet above sea level, to the eastern side of the range.

" Before going further, let us premise that Bute Inlet is the point on the Pacific coast which it is most desirable for the line to reach in order, at some future and not far distant period, to bring Vancouver Island and Victoria into direct communication with the interior of the continent. Taking it for granted that a practicable route does exist from the Tête Jaune Cache, *via* the North Fraser and Fort George, to Bute Inlet (a distance of four hundred and fifty miles), or from the Tête Jaune Cache to the same point, *via* Lac la Hache (also four hundred and fifty miles)—both distances taken from Progress Report of 1872, see page 17—we shall at once discuss the merits of that section of the Canada Pacific comprised between Portage la Prairie (Manitoba) and the Cache.

" From Portage la Prairie, in a north-west direction, and for a distance of about two hundred and twenty miles, the projected route passes over a very fine country. In the vicinity of the pretty poplar-wooded Riding Mountains, to the south, and almost within reach of the beautiful Lake Dauphin, and over the Swan River, until, when between the Thunder and Porcupine Hills, it takes a westward course for the Saskatchewan, distant a hundred and ninety-two miles. We shall now make the Thunder Hill a common point of departure for the two routes under discussion, for east of that prominence the line has passed over the best available ground. Resuming, then, our course for the Tête Jaune Cache, we strike almost due west for a hundred and ninety-two miles over a very easy country, but for the most part open, sparsely wooded, and containing many lakes, of which the waters are saturated with the sulphate of soda. From the crossing of the South Saskatchewan to that of the northern branch of the same river, at the White Mud Creek, above Edmonton, three hundred and fifty miles of country are crossed, nine-tenths of which is a treeless prairie, exposed to the fury of the cold northern blasts, rough and broken in many places, where good fresh water, excepting in the vicinity of the rivers, is extremely scarce; salt and brackish lakes are of frequent occurrence, and very much frequented by the nomadic tribes of the plains.

"Crossing the North Saskatchewan, we now leave the open plain country, and enter a vast swampy region, which, with the exception of some few dry ridges, extends to the Athabaska River. As a matter of course, this tract of country, which the line intersects for a distance of some one hundred and seventy miles, is wet, cold, and quite unsuitable for successful settlement. From the southern end of

Lac Brulé, which we have now reached, about one hundred miles take us to the Cache, which distance can be overcome by easy grades. A great portion of the section of country just described offers immense tracts of fine land, suitable, so far as the soil itself is concerned, for both agricultural and grazing purposes. But the drawbacks already briefly referred to—namely, the scarcity of wood and water—are insuperable obstacles in the way of successful and permanent settlement. It is true that occasionally small copses of poplars (the trees rarely exceeding eight inches in diameter) are met with; nevertheless, the extent of wooded compared with prairie land is so disproportionate, that but a widely-scattered community of settlers would be needed to clear off all the available timber in a very few years.

"On the score of fuel, it may be urged that the coal, which underlies a great extent of the Upper Saskatchewan country, may offer a good substitute for wood, and be used to advantage. There is no doubt that coal, in quantity enormous, but in quality, perhaps, doubtful, is to be found, especially west of Fort Pitt; but those who seek these regions with a view to settlement cannot be expected to turn all their attention and devote all their energies towards the painful and laborious extraction from the bowels of the earth of the wherewithal to keep body and soul together, during the long and severe winters which are the rule, when the thermometer often sinks to 40 deg. below zero. It is one thing to cross those beautiful prairies during the summer season, when the hills and dales are in the full flush of exuberant verdure, another to travel them in winter, in face of the biting northern blasts which sweep the boundless wastes of these interminable plains with a rigour and severity almost Arctic in their intensity.

"We shall now return to the Thunder Hill, the point where the proposed route to the Pacific, *via* Lac la Biche and Peace River, branches northwards from the one just described. Travelling west northwesterly for about one hundred and fifty miles, within the limits of the true forest, we reach Fort à la Corne. Somewhere in this vicinity, a crossing of the Saskatchewan must be sought; and gaining the north side of that river, the line of route would cross the Netsetting River, and, keeping south of Green and Pelican Lakes, seek the easiest way to Lac la Biche, through a thick wood country, supporting a growth of spruce, larch and poplars, abounding in lakes teeming with fish, and removed from the presence of the roving Indians of the plains. From Lac la Biche (in latitude 55 deg. north, where wheat has been successfully cultivated for years) to the western extremity of Lesser Slave Lake, is a distance of about one hundred and seventy miles, through a fairly level country, covered with forest.

This section is comparatively unknown, but, from Indian reports, is presumed to be level. From this point sixty-five miles of fine gently-rolling timbered country will take the line to the Smoky River, which can be crossed some thirty miles from its mouth. From the last-mentioned river the line would intersect and open up a vast and fertile region, situated to the south of the great Peace River—a region probably comprising an area equal in extent to Manitoba, well wooded, with abundance of fresh water, of excellent soil, and in all probability possessing unlimited quantities of good coal. The general elevation of this large tract of country is about one thousand eight hundred feet above sea level. The climate is most salubrious, and, by all accounts, as mild, if not milder, than that of Red River. On the extensive plains bordering upon the Peace River, both north and south of it, snow rarely exceeds two feet in depth, and never packs. Up to the month of December, the plains are often nearly bare; and although winter usually sets in with the month of November, the early opening of the spring in April compensates for the short fall.

"I shall here give several extracts from a letter written by a gentleman of reliability, who has lived in the Peace River country for seven years. Speaking of the climate, he says:—

"'Le climat est certainement salubre. Les vents qui règnent en maître ne sont généralement pas froids ; ils soufflent presque toujours de l'ouest à l'est, et du sud-ouest au nord-est. Les orages ne font point de dégats. En hiver même, la température est très variée, ce n'est que dans le mois de Janvier et une partie de Mars que quand le vent est nord, il fait bien froid.

"'A Athabasca, au contraire, le froid est intense et de longue durée. *La neige n'atteint ordinairement pas plus que deux pieds, encore n'est elle pas dure, l'air étant toujours sec et le ciel serein.*

"'Dans les côtes, dans les prairies, la nature offre une foule de fruits que les Européens même ne dédaigneraient pas sur leurs tables. Des poires, des cerises sauvages, des pembina, des raisins d'ours, des fraises, des framboises. . . . Il me semble que le pommier réussirait. L'orge mûrit tous les ans. Je pense que le blé semé en automne mûrirait très souvent, comme le blé du printemps. Une année j'ai semé des haricots le 24 de Mai, le 30 de Juillet ils étaient bons à manger. Les pois réussissent généralement, légumes toujours bien.'

"Of the mineral resources, he says :—'In many places tar exudes from the ground. The purest and whitest of salt can be collected in enormous quantities. Pure sulphur is found below Fort Vermilion. Bituminous springs abound, while the Smoky River, as its name indicates, proves the existence of vast beds of pit coal.'

"This magnificent country, rich in mineral wealth,

with abundance of timber, possessing millions of acres of the finest pasture land, watered by numerous small rivers, is intersected by the noble Peace River, navigable from the Rocky Mountain Portage to the Smoky River (a distance of two hundred and fifty miles), and probably very much further, for the largest river steamers.

"We shall now, once more, pick up the line of route, and keeping a little south of west, cross the Rocky Mountains by the Pine River Summit Lake Pass, if it be practicable. If, on the contrary, insurmountable obstacles impede our progress in that direction, we must keep to the right, heading the Pine River sufficiently to enable us to cross it at the most eligible point, and make for the Peace River Valley, by following which, and making a detour of one hundred and twenty-five miles, we shall reach McLeod Lake, after having passed through the Rocky Mountains at an elevation rarely exceeding one thousand eight hundred feet above the sea. This detour may, however, necessitate very heavy works of construction, the Pine River, owing to its deep valley, being itself, probably, the first serious obstacle. Between this river and the upper end of the Portage, probably thirty miles, the country is a dense forest, and apparently rough. The White Fish River has, besides, perhaps to be crossed. Above the Portage, and partly within the mountains, there are sixty or seventy miles of rough and expensive road to be constructed. Occasional level terraces can be made use of; but precipitous mountain sides, especially above the "Rapide Qui ne Parle Pas," will occasion heavy and expensive work, while the tortuousness of the river may require many bridges.

"The waters of the Peace River above the Portage being, however, navigable for stern-wheel steamers of light draught, some slight improvement being made at the Finlay Rapids, as far as the outlet of McLeod Lake, would greatly simplify the operation of road making, by furnishing cheap and easy means of transport along one hundred and forty-five miles of the line of route. From McLeod Lake, or its vicinity, one hundred and forty miles of country, chiefly unavailable for farming purposes, in some places rough, for a great part level, and probably nowhere exceeding two thousand four hundred feet above the sea, will bring the line to West Arm or Black River, whence the famed Chilcoten Valley, and thence the Bute Inlet may be reached.

"When we consider that the line just pointed out is *via* the Pine River Summit Lake Pass only fifty miles longer than that by the Tête Jaune Cache, or, the Pine Pass being impracticable, that the route *via* the circuitous Peace River Valley and the Parsnip only exceeds by one hundred and eighty miles the Yellow Head Pass route, that it will pass out of the region of deep snow, and open up the best and most available country of the Nor'-West for settlement, avoiding much rough country and the hideous Fraser River altogether, there can be no doubt as to the most eligible line for the great Interoceanic highway, to give it the conditions essential to its success as a commercial and political undertaking.

CANADIAN PACIFIC RAILWAY ROUTE,
via Tête Jaune Cache.

Route.	Remarks.	Elevation.	Miles.
From Portage la Prairie to Thunder Hill....	Fine country for settlement......		220
From Thunder Hill to the crossing of the South Saskatchewan......	Much open country, salt lakes, little wood......		192
From South Saskatchewan to the crossing near the White Mud....	Nearly all open country, salt lakes, hilly, and much exposed		350
From White Mud to South end of Lac Brule...........	Swampy, cold, unfitted for settlement.............		170
From Lac Brule to the Tete Jaune Cache............	Unsuitable for agriculture..............	3760 ft	110
From Tete Jaune Cache to Bute Inlet, either by Lac la Hache, or the North Fraser River and Fort George and Chilcoten...........	The Chilcoten Valley is the only available district for settlement in this section............		450
			1492

53 miles shorter than the Peace River route, *via* Pine River Summit Lake.

178 miles shorter than the route through the Peace River Valley.

CANADIAN PACIFIC RAILWAY ROUTE, via Peace River.

Route.	Remarks.	Miles.
From Portage la Prairie to Thunder Hill	Fine country for settlement	220
From Thunder Hill to Fort a la Corne	Fine country, for the most part wooded	150
From Fort a la Corne to Lac la Biche	Thick wood country, many lakes abounding in fish	350
From Lac la Biche to west end of Lesser Slave Lake	Wooded country, not much known, but reported level	170
From west end of Lesser Slave Lake to Smoky River	Fine country, well wooded and watered	65
From Smoky River to Pine River Summit Lake	Beautiful country, prairie, woods, coal	170
From Pine River Summit Lake to Lake McLeod	Not available for agriculture	60
From Lake McLeod to Quesnel	Very little of it available for agriculture	140
From Quesnel to Bute Inlet, via Chilcoten	(?)	220
		1,545

APPENDIX I.

THE INDIANS OF BRITISH COLUMBIA.

IT MAY be of interest to offer a few remarks regarding the Indian population of British Columbia, a passing allusion to the aboriginal inhabitants of the nor'-west coast of the Dominion being all the more deserving of notice from the fact that they very much outnumber the white population of that Province.

The population of this interesting race in the Province is estimated at about thirty thousand, but from the extreme difficulty of taking a correct census in such a vast and rugged country as British Columbia, those figures may be taken as merely approximate. One cannot but be struck with the Mongolian cast of countenance of the coast Indians of British Columbia. Also among the tribes with whom it is not customary to alter the cranial formation by pressure in infancy, the skull is found to possess the flat central ridge peculiar to the Mongolian races.

Within the memory of the Hudson's Bay "oldest inhabitants" in this region, Japanese junks have been known to drift across in a disabled state. What more natural than to suppose that this portion of the Pacific Coast was either populated by that means, or that in former times those visitors left their impress on the aboriginal race? There is another mixture in the blood on the west coast of Vancouver Island, and a very marked one—the Spanish, owing to the Spaniards having long ago had a settlement at Nootka. Strangely enough, the Spanish cast of countenance does not show in the women, who have the same flat features as their sisters to the eastward. Nor is it so noticeable among the young men, many of whom, however, have beards, a most unusual appendage among American Indians, and of course traceable to the cause referred to. The features are more observable among the older men, many of whom, with their long, narrow, pointed faces and beards, would, if washed, present very fair models for Don Quixote.

A point of some interest in speculating on the origin of the present inhabitants is, that in several parts of the Province there are spots thickly strewn with stone cairns. Many of these have been opened by parties of gentlemen interested in such subjects, and have been found, in every case, to contain human remains. The Indians are very jealous of any desecration of their dead, but they had no objection to these researches, observing "That they did not belong to their people." The present natives never bury their dead. Until very lately incremation was general among the northern Indians, but they, in common with many other tribes, now box up their dead in highly ornamented chests, curiously carved and painted, and place them in small huts at a short distance from their villages. Others again put the deceased in his canoe, with all his hunting necessaries, and trice him up into a tree. This strong apparent difference suggests a pre-existing race.

These people are spread all over the seaboard and inland waters. Owing to the thick and impenetrable forest which covers the country down to the very water's edge, they have been driven to subsist principally by fishing. There are several distinct languages, large groups of small tribes speaking dialects of the same language. To furnish an instance of the numerous sub-divisions into which the British Columbian Indian race has been split up, some of those tribes inhabiting the country adjacent to the Skeena may be instanced: the Babine Indians, the Kissgarrase, the Culdoah, Kyspyox, Kittumarks, Kitsigeuchly, Kitwangar, Kitsellase, Kitwuncole, Killoosa, and further down the Skeena, the Kitsumkalum. These enumerated belong, with the exception of the Babines, to the Skeena. On the Naas and its tributaries, and in fact on every inlet of the coast, the subdivisions are just as frequent.

Although, however, the same dialect may be common to many, they do not seem to be bound together by acknowledged relationship or alliance. It is perhaps as well for the white population, which is scanty, and the settlers away from the main towns, who are few and very far between, that among the Indians it is, most emphatically, "every one for himself." They are split up into innumerable small tribes, there being a village or ranche in nearly every indentation or inlet on this much broken coast. Each has its chief, who does not seem to possess much authority, and many have intertribal feuds of long standing.

Besides the right of fishing in the waters immediately surrounding their settlement, each tribe has, in common with several others, a right to share in the salmon and "Oolahan" fishing which takes place annually at the nearest river or inlet where the fish run up at certain seasons. On these occasions there is sometimes a jollification in the form of a whisky feast, and when mad drunk with the poison sold by some white ruffian, against the law, murders are often committed. If the murderer belongs to a different tribe from that of the victim, it at once becomes a family question, and on the first opportunity a life will be taken on the other side, and so on, backwards and forwards, for the retaliation may not square the account. Their idea of arithmetic is most limited, and the consequence is that these feuds become interminable.

As the people of British Columbia object to their fellow subjects carrying on these "little games," and as, moreover, all these Indians are thievish and treacherous, and would think nothing of killing the white settlers leading solitary lives at great distances from civilization, the majesty of the law takes the form of *man-of-war* visitations. For a long time two small British war steamers have been detached from the Pacific Squadron for this special service. A periodical run up and down the coast by one of these gunboats has a very salutary effect. It is strange how the movements of these ships are known among all the Indians. The fact of the "Sparrowhawk" leaving for the north was always known before her arrival; there is no communication except by canoe, and yet she invariably found herself "expected." The special duties of these ships consist in their acting as the police of the coast, more particularly of the inland waters, in preventing the sale of spirituous liquors among the natives; in impressing them with the feeling that they are being watched over; in the protection of outlying settlers; in the adjustment of disputes, and the prevention of bloody quarrels among the different tribes, and, in some cases, in rendering assistance at shipwrecks on the dangerous west coast of Vancouver Island. The Indians there are among the finest specimens, physically, of the whole British Columbian coast. Splendid boatmen, they venture out in their fine canoes to great distances in pursuit of fur seals and sea-otters. They are more treacherous, bloodthirsty, savage and bold than those in the more placid inland waters, perhaps from the fact that they receive fewer visits and therefore know that their misdeeds are less likely to be found out.

Some years ago the "Sutlej" frigate shelled one of the villages, the Ahowsett, for an outrage on a small trading craft. Of course the Indians all cleared out into the bush and the casualties were small. Subsisting, however, as they do, almost entirely on fish, the destruction of their canoes is a fearful punishment. It would be easy to exterminate them all in that way. The "Sutlej's" shell, however, did some damage in the long run, as several unexploded ones having been found in the forest in the rear of the village, some of the ingenious Indians proceeded to extract the fuzes with cold chisels to get at the powder, the natural result being that some half a dozen of them came to grief.

In the beginning of 1869, a British lumber ship sailed from a port in Puget Sound. Not very long afterwards a trader on the west coast found the wreck of a ship on the beach at Hesquot. On going along the beach he found a number of headless skeletons, which raised his suspicions. After a careful search he found the remains of what had evidently been a very large man, also headless, but still the flesh clothed the bones sufficiently for him to notice that the body had a hole through it as of a bullet-wound. He also found the skull of a woman and part of her body. On his inquiring of the Hesquot Indians what all this meant, they told him that the ship had been wrecked, and that all the bodies had drifted on shore headless. He reported the fact with his suspicions of foul play on his return to Victoria, and the result was the sending of H.M.S. "Sparrowhawk" to investigate the matter, two magistrates going in her. On her arrival a number of the Indians surrounded the ship in their canoes, from among whom the trader, who accompanied the expedition as interpreter and witness, selected a number whom he suspected; they were ordered on board and kept prisoners, while a body of armed marines landed as a protection to the magistrates and medical officer. The village was searched for any of the clothing or property of the unfortunate crew, and some papers, logs, etc., were found, which proved the vessel to have been the "John Bright." The party then proceeded to the scene of the wreck, where the remains were exhumed, and medical testimony was taken before a coroner's jury formed from those present. The jury afterwards sat on board, and the suspected Indians with their Tyhees, or chiefs, were examined, but nothing could be elicited beyond the fact of the wreck. Every one was morally convinced that murder had been committed, but how was it to be brought home to any among all those faces of injured innocence, all swearing black and blue that the sea was responsible for it all. Nothing was found out the first day. One juror, a burly pioneer of civilization, who had gone round in the capacity of special constable and grave-digger, was strenuous and earnest in his advice to Captain Mist to "clear them darned skunks out," that "they had all had a finger in the pie." It appeared he had been on a "prospecting tour" among those fellows before, and could not say much for their morals. Knowing their superstitions he went down that evening to smoke his pipe in the engine-room, which had been turned into a jail for the nonce, and sitting down by one of the high-flavoured red blanketed individuals—one who had some experience of civilization and could speak a little English, he began at him : "Now, John, what's the use of your keeping dark about all this? We know all about it! and that's why we're here; a little bird came to Victoria and told our big medicine-man (the Doctor of the 'Sparrowhawk') all about it! Now, come, 'dilett wawa' (speak straight)!" John glared in horror and said he would "speak straight," and then pointing to another red-blanketed statue, sitting on its haunches, he said, "That's the man who killed the captain." The other fellow immediately rapped out, "And that man," pointing back, "is the one who killed the captain's wife." The next morning the whole tribe swore to this, their story being that the crew left the ship in a boat, leaving the captain, whose leg was broken, on board with his wife. The ship drifted on shore, and they landed either by the small boat, which capsized on beaching, or on a piece of the poop. The captain was shot by Katkeena, and on his wife running for protection to the old chief, John shot her. The two were tried at Victoria, and sentenced to death. They were taken back in the " Sparrowhawk," and executed in the presence of the whole of the men of the tribe, who seemed rather pleased than otherwise. The mystery of the absent heads was probably explained by an account which came in a very roundabout way from a tribe in Washington Territory. It appeared that at a "potlatch" or feast some Hesquots told the story. The ship drifted ashore in a gale, and the crew deserted in the long-boat, leaving the captain and his wife, who landed alone, apparently. The Indians said to each other, "Come, there are only two left; if we kill them, we can take everything out of the ship, and they won't know anything about it in Victoria. The unfortunate couple were then murdered, but at that moment the crew came out of the bush, having succeeded in landing a little further north. To conceal the first murder, which would probably never have been committed had they known there were so many survivors, they massacred all the remainder, tied stones to their necks and threw them into deep water. The chafing, assisted by decomposition, having worked the heads off, the headless trunks floated ashore. To this day the fate of the unfortunate children of the captain and that of their nurse, is a mystery, for none of their remains were found. Rumours of little white girls among the Indians came to Victoria once or twice, but nothing definite could be traced.

The Governor often goes in one of the ships on a tour among the different tribes. On these occasions disputes between the natives, or between the Indians and the miners, are settled. It was on an official tour of this kind that the late Governor Seymour died on board the "Sparrowhawk." Shortly before his death he succeeded in effecting a peace between two tribes who had been applying the rules of subtraction in an unscientific manner to each other for some time. The ceremony took place on board, and is described as interesting. Whisky was at the bottom of the row, as it most generally is, and strangely enough, the individual who supplied the stuff was captured a few days before in his schooner. The occasion was a marriage between a Chimpsean and a Nishka woman. A whisky feast followed, and during the firing of guns and pistols, a Chimpsean was shot. His people cleared out, vowing vengeance, which they took some time after, by killing two Nishkas, whom they caught fishing off the mouth of the Naas. Now, of course, the Nishkas considered that the debt was the other way, and took an early opportunity of securing repayment and something more. So things had gone on till one tribe had taken some half-a-dozen more lives than the other, and accounts were considerably complicated. It was at this juncture that the Governor arrived. The difficulty of getting one tribe to go to the other's village was overcome somehow, and the Nishka principal men went down to Fort Simpson. On the following morning a large number of Chimpsean canoes, with banners flying, went off to the "Sparrowhawk" The Nishkas were ranged along the starboard side of the deck, and the Chimpseans were placed facing them. Of course the Europeans looked on with considerable curiosity, and, no doubt, through their ignorance of the language, lost a rare treat of flowery and figurative eloquence. After a considerable period of silence, accompanied by an apparently indifferent scrutiny of each other, a grunt came from the starboard side, which was quickly responded to from the port. Then sonorous, soft and lispy sentences again from the Nishkas, answered by one or two "hah's," with dignified and ponderous nods. Gradually arms began to be raised, and the speeches flowed low, dignified and monotonous, answered by sententious nods, and listened to in deep silence and with wrapt attention. Every one was heard to the end without interruption. After considerable "speechification" on both sides, an agreement was come to as to how many blankets were to be given by the tribe which had taken most lives, as compensation to the other tribe. Ten blankets is generally considered the price of a man's life in Indian currency. The ratification of the treaty of peace then took place—a herald advanced from each side with a dried sea-lion's throat filled with swan's down, and proceeded to smear each one of the opposite party with a handful of it, each one taking off his hat to undergo the operation, till they all looked as if covered with snow flakes. This is the Indian symbol of peace, and they all wear the down till it drops off. Each chief affixed his mark to a document, which was drawn up and sealed in the presence of the Governor, after which they all sat down together to a collation of tea, molasses and ship's biscuits—a clay pipe and leaf of tobacco being served out to each to finish off with. Their idea of tea is peculiar, as they mix it half-and-half with molasses! The Nishkas landed afterwards as guests of the Chimpseans.

In the olden days the commanders of the gunboats used to deal out summary justice to a much greater extent than is done now, and with very good effect, generally, as it is absurd to wade with judge, jury and a full court of lawyers through a slough of barefaced lying. The "cat" was found a most effectual means of reforming thieves. There is rather an amusing story told of that period. A gun-boat, commanded by a fine fellow, since dead—a man who did much for the colony in its infancy—got into a hornet's nest on one occasion, and finding it perfectly useless to remain under the heavy fire of enemies concealed in the bush, backed out. So narrow was the creek that she could not turn. Like sensible men, they made a virtue of necessity, and only an idiot would have accused them of showing the white feather. At this time, as is often the case in new, and, perhaps, particularly in mining countries, the principal occupant of the editorial chair, in Victoria, was somewhat given to use his pen like a Southern Islander's war-club, instead of a surgeon's knife. This Jehu, or, perhaps, more truly Phaeton, who drove the curricle of the press much to his own satisfaction, must needs make merry on this, and served up a highly-flavoured and considerably hashed account of the affair, laying great and undue stress on the "discretion" part of valour, and thereby very nearly caught a tartar. The editor was politely asked to lunch with the bespattered captain, and guilelessly went. The ship had steam up, and started immediately on his arrival, when something strange in the preparations on deck attracted his notice, and swiftly roused his suspicions. *They were rigging the gratings*, and he was going to have a hot lunch, but it was to be on his own back! He was off like a flash of lightning overboard and swimming for the shore. Of course the law was brought into play, and the captain had to pay heavy damages. Still it is a question whether he did not chuckle over the fright of our gallant quill driver. Lucky for him that his story did not end with nine tails!

By all accounts the Indians of the coast, as well as those inhabiting the interior of British Columbia, are steadily decreasing in numbers. The ravages of disease, and the immoderate use of bad whisky, which, despite the efforts of the preventive service, is yet dealt out to them in great quantities, are doubtless the causes. Their reckless, filthy, and loose mode of living must also tend to shorten their days. Eruptive complaints carry them off by scores. The fearful quantities of oolahan grease which they devour, to an extent incredible to those who have not witnessed their feats of gluttony, would, I should think, be cause sufficient for the speedy dissolution of any decently-constructed white man. I have known my own Indians (those travelling with me) devour two or three pounds of rancid grease at a meal, the stench of which was worse than that of any slaughter-house.

The inland Indians, though they live under very different circumstances to those of the coast, present the same Mongolian cast of features, and resemble the latter in many other points.

The Indian population is much more numerous on the seaboard than in the interior. Between the

British American boundary line and Sitka, Alaska, I believe the coast to be quite as numerously peopled as further south ; but there, the Indians do not enjoy the same privileges as their Columbian brothers do, for the Americans are too apt to apply the same rules on the west coast of North America, as they have hitherto been guided by in their relations with the plain tribes.'

APPENDIX II.

ON THE TOPOGRAPHY, CLIMATE AND GEOLOGY OF THE WESTERN LIMIT OF THE FERTILE BELT, WITH SOME REMARKS UPON THE ROCKY MOUNTAINS AND THE PEACE RIVER.

BEFORE entering into a brief description of the Peace River country, or the western portion of the Fertile Belt of the British Nor'-West, some remarks may be offered upon that portion of British territory lying north of the Rocky Mountain House, and west of the North Saskatchewan.

The Rocky Mountain House (latitude fifty-two degrees, twenty-one minutes) is nicely situated on the left bank of the North Saskatchewan upon a wide and level shingle terrace. It is one of the most securely built of the Hudson Bay Company's establishments, and is of quadrangular form, with high and strong palisades outside the dwelling-houses and other offices. Viewed from the exterior, the appearance of this fort is anything but inviting;

it resembles a moderately sized gaol more than anything else, and the narrow, strongly-protected entrance, with one or two diminutive side-doors, and an occasional sliding wicket, suggest very forcibly the precautions which the inhabitants consider advisable in their dealings with the Blackfeet, who are the principal frequenters of this trading post. These gentry, when they make their periodical visits for the purposes of trade and barter, generally pitch their tents in close proximity to the establishment. When I last visited the Rocky Mountain House, in the November of 1871, there were twenty-five lodges of Piegan Indians in from the plains, who thronged the courtyard inside, and required very careful supervision to prevent the exercise of their thieving propensities, which are very strong. On this occasion I photographed a group of the principal men amongst them.

Looking westward from the fort, a few distant peaks of the Rocky Mountains are visible here and there above the top of the thick forest which covers the Saskatchewan Valley and the neighbouring foot hills. A few hundred yards below, the river takes a sudden bend northwards, and the Clearwater, a beautiful mountain stream, well worthy of the appropriate name it bears, enters it. From the Rocky Mountain House to the Brazeau Range, and past the latter to the commencement of the Kootanie Plains, distant about ninety-five miles, the furthest point I

have reached in this direction, the features of the
Saskatchewan Valley and adjoining country are
rough, and travelling, either on foot or on horseback,
is very irksome and laborious, owing to the hilly
nature of the country, the numerous swamps, and large
burnt tracts through which the trails are cut. The
scenery, however, is very beautiful, especially between the Bighorn Creek and White Goat River,
and can hardly be surpassed elsewhere in the mountains for rugged grandeur. Further on, in the very
heart of the mountains, the Saskatchewan derives its
waters from some immense glaciers. The mountain
valleys are quite filled up at this point by a huge
mer de glace many miles in extent, above which, at
irregular intervals, rocky and fantastically-shaped
peaks stand up like islands in the midst of an eter-
nally frozen sea. The eastern portion of this immense ice field abuts upon a beautiful lake several
miles in extent, the shores of which are covered with
forest down to the very water's edge, while immediately behind, huge mountains, elevated six thousand feet above the blue waters of this ice-fed lake,
stand up in all the pride of their sullen grandeur.
East of this glacier lake is the Howe's Pass, by
which, at one time, hopes were entertained that the
Canada Pacific Railway might pass. As one might
naturally be led to imagine, the climate of this Upper Saskatchewan country is not by any means a
genial one, and if my memory serves me aright, I

saw the mercury indicate thirty degrees below zero on the morning of the 9th of November, 1871, when camped just within the Brazeau range. The Saskatchewan River, at the Rocky Mountain House, is about one hundred and thirty yards wide, and its valley displays sandstone cliffs, in which occasional coal seams appear. From this point for a considerable distance northward, this appears to me to form the boundary between the Fertile Belt and the cold, swampy and broken country which extends westward to the base of the Rocky Mountains.

To my thinking the western and northern line of the Fertile Belt would, taking the Rocky Mountain House for a starting point, follow the Saskatchewan to the White Mud river, thence northerly almost to Fort Assiniboine, from the latter to the outlet of Lesser Slave Lake, and keeping this sheet of water for its southern line of demarcation, strike west by south over the Smoky River, almost to the base of the Rocky Mountains, or to, say, the one hundred and twentieth and a-half degree of west longitude, then north for one hundred miles, and then eastward to the Athabasca, at the point where the Clearwater enters that stream ; finally, a south-east course would bring it to the Saskatchewan, slightly east of Fort à la Corne. All the country, or nearly all, to the west and north of this rather curiously curved line may be set down as of no great importance for cultivation. The southern boundary of this zone is difficult to define, the forty-ninth parallel may suffice for present purposes, but will include much unfertile, arid, and treeless country, totally unfitted for permanent habitation.

The gradual dip northward of the continent immediately east of the Rocky Mountains is something remarkable. Its general elevation near the Rocky Mountain House is about three thousand three hundred feet above sea level, while at Fort Assiniboine two thousand two hundred feet may be taken as the level of the high land behind the fort, and at the Peace River, one thousand eight hundred feet is about the maximum elevation. The greater part of the belt of country drained by the western tributaries of the North Saskatchewan and by the Athabasca and its affluents, as far north as Lesser Slave Lake, and east to the longitude of Fort Assiniboine, may be fairly set down as valueless for cultivation. It is a cold and swampy tract of country, considerably elevated, and much of it mountainous. Between the Smoky River and the Athabasca, some very high hills, probably offshoots of the Rocky Mountains, stretch eastwards until within thirty miles of Lesser Slave Lake; one of these spurs, that more immediately to the south, I crossed at an elevation of about three thousand five hundred feet above the sea. Another and still higher spur lay fifteen miles to the northwest, and between them the Swan River flowed on its way towards the Lesser Slave Lake. A more forlorn piece of country than that lying between Fort Assiniboine and Lesser Slave Lake cannot well be imagined: a tract of broken rocky land, covered with swamps, and valueless for every purpose but the chase.

In the bed of the Swan River, elevated, probably, two thousand five hundred feet above the sea, at the place we forded it, a lignite seam, twenty-four inches in thickness, was seen. This was, doubtless, the connecting link between the lignites of the Saskatchewan and the strata more to the north. This formation (lignite) extends over a vast area of the Nor'-West, having been recognized on the southern branches of the South Saskatchewan, as well as on the Athabasca and its tributaries, and the Mackenzie and other rivers flowing into it. The meridian of 111 degrees west longitude may be assumed as the eastern boundary of the lignite formation of the British Nor'-West, although lignite strata were long ago discovered on the Souris River, at a place known to the half-breeds as La Roche Percée. This locality is about seven miles north of the forty-ninth parallel or boundary line, and in longitude 104 degrees west; but the seams there probably belong to the Missouri tertiary lignite basin. Four thin seams are here mentioned by Dr. Hector, and some of them were apparently very fine in quality, and had much the appearance of cannel coal. The stratum seen at the Swan River appeared to be of an inferior kind, and burned with difficulty. About sixty miles west of the Swan River, there must be immense quantities of coal on the Smoky River; for that stream, for many miles of its course, presents the extraordinary appearance of a "black country," owing to frequent clouds of smoke arising from the combustion of the mineral upon its banks, and in the vicinity.

On proceeding a little more to the north, and on gaining the watershed of the Peace River, a decided change is at once perceptible, not only in the appearance of the country, but also in the climate. After passing the little belt of swampy ground lying between Lesser Slave Lake and the Peace River, the ground dips gently; and on gaining the edge of the valley of the latter stream, the general elevation of the land appears to be only seventeen hundred feet above the sea level, and perhaps is even less.

Within an area bounded by the Smoky River, the Rocky Mountains and the parallel of $56\frac{1}{2}$ degrees north latitude, there lies the future garden of the West, now lying fallow, but yet gorgeous with many of the choicest prairie flowers, and replete with the finest wild fruits peculiar to both woods and plain. Beneath its serene sky, the lovely hills and dales, with many crystal mountain-fed rivulets between, afford the choicest soil on the continent, from which the husbandman will eventually extract with ease abundant harvests. In this favoured spot, sheltered on the west by the majestic peaks of the finest mountain range of the North American Continent, there appears to be a singularly happy distribution of prairie and wooded land. Here you have magnificent rough-bark poplars and spruce of immense size; there, within a stone's-throw almost, an undulating prairie. Immense treasures of fuel lie but a little way beneath the surface, awaiting the advent of the pioneer of civilization, the snorting steam-horse, to be conveyed eastward, for the use of the less fortunate dwellers of the Saskatchewan and Manitoba. Through the very heart of this "happy valley," the noble Peace River presents one of the finest natural channels of inland navigation to be seen on the continent, by which easy communication with the northern sea might be opened if necessary, and the products of the rich fisheries of the Arctic easily and economically conveyed to the South and East. In connection with this matter of northern fisheries, it may here be stated that, if the Canada Pacific road be eventually pushed through the Peace River country, a branch road of three hundred and fifty miles in length, over a very easy and level country, would suffice to bring to the main line, with but one transhipment, the cargoes of the largest sea-going vessels.

A few miles below the mouth of the Smoky River the land is very much cut up by deep gullies—the result of erosion on the argillaceous strata—which extend to a great depth below the surface of all the Peace River country. All the tributaries of the Peace River present the same characteristics, cutting deeper and deeper through the clayey banks, until, at their junction with the parent stream, they emerge through ravines six or seven hundred feet in depth. On the north side of the Peace River, between the site of the old Fort and Dunvegan, the country is nearly perfectly level, with here and there a few erratics strewn over the surface. The sloping valley banks are occasionally rough, and some of the most curiously-formed conical mounds of gravel occupy the slopes. On the south side, the more undulating nature of the surface, with occasional mounds and ridges, attests the bygone action of the sea. At the site of the old Fort, opposite Smoky River, there are several fine level terraces; but generally, between that and Dunvegan, the valley slopes irregularly to the water, often displaying sandstone cliffs, ruinous and broken, and sometimes several hundred feet in height. The bed of the Peace River is for the most part strewn with numerous boulders and gravel of lime stone and sandstone (the latter often forming most excellent whet-stones), while above St. John's the detached slabs of sandstone, which are found in profusion along the water's edge, afford the best of grindstones. The country thirty or forty miles south of the Peace River is described as far superior to that we passed through. The half-breed hunters and residents about Dunvegan speak of it with rapture. There they can roam on horseback over vast stretches of prairie in pursuit of game, which supplies the scanty Indian population with food. They speak of delightful lakelets of fresh water, almost hidden from view by the luxuriant foliage of the sylvan groves in which they are sometimes situated, while numerous flocks of feathered game dot the surface of their tranquil waters.

The climate of this favoured land is singularly mild, notwithstanding its high latitude; but a few very simple causes may be assigned for this apparent anomaly. The immediate proximity of the Rocky Mountains to windward is an important element to be taken into account in considering the climate. For one effect of mountain ranges being to drain the winds which cross them of their moisture, it follows that the warm breezes of the Pacific partially lose the moisture with which they are saturated, while crossing the elevated and snowy peaks of the Rocky Mountains, and reach the low country to the east, divested in great measure of their protecting screen of vapour. This abstraction of moisture exposes the places to leeward more fully to the influence of terrestrial and solar radiation. Hotter summers and colder but drier winters are the natural result. The high hills south of the Smoky River also act in the same way, by intercepting the vapours which accompany the south-west winds, and thus help to render the climate, probably, the best in the Nor'-West. The low gap in the Rocky Mountains, through which the Peace River flows eastward, also helps to mitigate the climate to leeward, by permitting, to a slight extent, the passage of the warm west winds, which tend to lessen the severity of the spring months, and melt the snows at a season when the eastern part of the continent is yet buried beneath its winter mantle. The early opening of the spring upon the Peace River is well established, not only by meteorological registers, but by the accounts of the present residents. On the other hand, the winter months are not a whit more severe than on the Saskatchewan or Red River, while the atmosphere is very much drier. Witness the fact that snow rarely exceeds two feet in depth, and never packs, thus offering wonderful facilities towards the economic maintenance of a railroad. Mr. Macoun, the botanist, who accompanied me through the country, states that the *flora* on the Peace River indicate a climate almost as warm as that of Belleville, in Ontario; and he further remarks that two-thirds of the species observed between Lesser Slave Lake and Fort St. John are identical with those of Ontario. Curiously enough, the north side of the Peace River Valley is generally bare of trees, while the southern slopes are thickly timbered. This is accounted for by the fact that the early effects of the spring sun are to speedily melt the snow, and the steep slopes, in consequence, soon suffer from want of moisture. On the southern banks, however, from being kept much longer in the shade, moisture remains, and the growth of trees and other vegetation is thereby promoted to a greater extent. From Dunvegan to the Rocky Mountain Portage, the southern banks of the Peace River are generally densely wooded, and the forest gradually extends southwards, until, when behind Fort St. John, the wooded region is probably thirty or forty miles in width. The ground becomes rougher in the same ratio, and behind Fort St. John rises towards the mountains. The Indians, however, aver most emphatically that further south the prairie extends right up to the mountains, which, according to their accounts, exhibit prairie vegetation far up their eastern slopes. The north side of the Peace River is generally open, and although woods prevail to some extent, much prairie occupies the country even remote from the river, a fair horse trail taking the traveller from Dunvegan to Fort Vermilion in five or six days.

We shall now consider a very important subject, namely, the elevation above sea-level of the Peace River during its course through the country just described, and through the Rocky Mountains. The reader will bear in mind that the statistics I am now about to offer are derived more from *data* previously determined than from the meteorological observations taken by me during the journey. The high scientific authorities from whom those *data* emanate will be sufficient guarantee for the elevations of Dunvegan on the east, and Fort George on the west side of the Rocky Mountains.

Sir John Richardson, David Thompson, and Colonel Lefroy put the elevation of the former place, respectively, at seven hundred and eighty, one thousand, and nine hundred and ten feet above the sea. The Royal Engineers have estimated the altitude of the Fraser River at Fort George to be one thousand six hundred and ninety feet above sea. In my deductions as to the actual elevation of the Peace River between these points, I have made the datum level, not the mean of the three estimates of the altitude of Dunvegan, but the highest of the number, in order to ensure a result which, if proved erroneous (as it very likely is to some extent), after a careful system of levels, will be, at least, above the truth. The mean fall of the Peace River, from the foot of the Rocky Mountain Portage to Dunvegan (a distance estimated at one hundred and eighty miles), is assumed to be eighteen inches per mile, an allowance I really believe to be much too great. This gives the foot of the Rocky Mountain Portage an elevation of one thousand two hundred and seventy feet. Simultaneous observations of the atmospheric pressure at the foot and head of the Portage being impossible when I passed over it, a reliable estimate of the difference in level between these points has not been obtained; but, as nearly as I can judge, that difference is about two hundred and forty feet. Having judged the course of the river, from the Finlay Rapids to the head of the Rocky Mountain Canon, to be about seventy miles, and from the Finlay to the Little McLeod River seventy-five miles, those quantities, multiplied into twenty-four and eighteen inches respectively (the assumed descent of the main stream and south branch), place the elevation of the mouth of Little McLeod River at one thousand seven hundred and sixty-two feet; and assuming the level of Lake McLeod to be one thousand eight hundred feet above the sea, the difference (thirty-eight feet) may be taken as the fall of the Little River, a rapid stream, which, including Pack Lake, is about fourteen miles in length. A pretty fair barometric section was obtained from McLeod Lake to Lake Stewart, a distance of, say, eighty miles. Adopting one thousand eight hundred feet as the elevation of Lake Stewart, the section referred to fits in very well; and the fall of the Nacosla or Stewart River, from the lake of that name to its confluent point with the Fraser at Fort George, being estimated at one hundred feet, exactly satisfies the conditions required. But those deductions have been carefully checked throughout by the aneroid at every possible point, the variations of atmospheric pressure being taken into account, as far as possible; and so many precautions have been used in drawing inferences, that, unless some very grave error has crept in, the figures now given cannot be very far from the truth. The elevations are shown in the section, and are as follows, viz. :—

Dunvegan	1,000 feet above sea.	
Foot of Rocky Mountain Portage,	1,270 " " "	
Head " " "	1,510 " " "	
Finlay Branch	1,650 " " "	
McLeod Lake	1,800 " " "	
Stewart's Lake	1,800 " " "	

Before leaving the question of the elevations of the principal points on the Peace River, some remarks as to the adaptability of that river valley for a railroad line may be opportune. There is no doubt that this valley presents the lowest available pass in the Rocky Mountains for a line of communication from the East to the West. It has, however, one or two serious drawbacks—the circuitous route which it would oblige a railway to take, and the extreme roughness of some portions of the line, from the crossing of the Pine River until the mountains are passed altogether. These local difficulties may, however, not be so great as they appeared to me ; and if necessity should compel the roadway to be hewn out of the very mountain sides, while passing the heart of the range, yet I believe the avoidance of the Fraser River, and much more rough country through which it would be necessary to take a line *via* the Tête Jaune Cache, would more than compensate for the increased distance and heavy work of the Peace River Valley route.

But I believe that it may not be necessary to follow the Peace Valley at all. From many Indian reports which reached me, I am inclined to favour the belief that a pass or depression in the Rocky Mountains exists in about latitude fifty-five and a-half degrees north, and some thirty or forty miles south of the Portage Hill. Somewhere about this locality the Pine River is said to have its source in a lake which also sends its waters westward into the Parsnip or south branch of the Peace River. If this route be found practicable, then the line of road will not pass near the Peace River Valley at all, but will intersect the beautiful and partially prairie lands lying immediately south of it, and McLeod Lake will probably be reached by a route one hundred and twenty-five miles shorter than the other. This route which may or may not be practicable, I brought under the notice of the chief engineer of the Canada Pacific, upon my return to Ottawa last March, but whether or not steps have been taken to ascertain its feasibility, I do not know.

Having now briefly touched upon the topographical features of this section of the North-West, a few passing remarks on its geological characteristics may prove interesting to the reader. The Rocky Mountains within British territory may be said to lie about N.N.W., and S.S.E., and are composed of three distinct ranges, which appear to converge more closely as they extend northward, until at the great transverse trough through which the Peace River flows, they so dovetail into each other as to present the appearance of one huge longitudinal mass.

Although I have already referred to the Rocky Mountain Portage Hill as being a part of the outer range, yet, I think, it may be considered as forming but a portion of the foot hills, for westwardly, and for many miles higher up the Peace River, there are hardly any mountains worth mentioning, until within a short distance of the "Rapide qui ne parle pas." I am inclined to put the extreme breadth of the transverse section of the Rocky Mountains through which the Peace River flows at about thirty miles only. However, it is difficult to say where the hills end, and the actual mountains begin; at any rate the three great longitudinal valleys, so well defined in the more southern portions of the huge range, are with difficulty definable in the Peace River valley.

According to Dr Hector, and within the field of his explorations, immense thick-bedded strata of limestone, associated with fossils of Devonian or Carboniferous age, together with sandy shales, compose the first range. The same limestones and shales occur in the second range, and generally present a huge vertical wall to the westward. The third

P

range is composed of the carboniferous limestones resting on slates.

There is every reason to believe that the same geological features characterize that portion of the same general structure through which the Peace River flows, in so far, at least, as its component parts are concerned. Numerous fossils, two at least of which bore great resemblance to *Lonsdalia* and *Lithostrotion*, being seen on the banks of the Peace River amongst the numerous limestone boulders with which the river bed is strewn.

It is curious to speculate upon the physical features of this portion of the North American continent at the period when one continuous sea stretched from the Arctic southwards, and not only washed the eastern slopes of the Rocky Mountain range, but also filled the Peace River gap, a trough originally formed by dislocation and subsequent separation of the mountain masses.

A mile or so before reaching the upper end of the Rocky Mountain Portage, the traveller from the east passes over a series of well-defined terraces, three in number, which well mark ancient sea lines. A most curious fact in connection with these terraces is that the highest of the three, as far as I can remember, has about the same elevation above sea level as the country on the north side of the river, east of the Portage Hill.

It is possible, then, that, when the waters of the

ocean washed the upper terrace, the Portage Hill was a peninsula connected with the Bull's-head (a hill to the north) by the narrow strip of dry land where the traveller now attains his greatest elevation in making the portage. A sea level eighteen hundred feet higher than the present one would fulfil these conditions, and would also suffice to submerge the eastern Laurentian axis between Hudson's Bay and Lake Winnipeg, or at least convert it into a chain of islands. "At that time," according to Dr. Hector, "the coast line would have left the Rocky Mountains in latitude fifty-six degrees N. near Peace River, and have followed what is now the watershed between the Saskatchewan and the rivers flowing more to the north, till it reached the one hundred and seventh degree west longitude. From this point the Thickwood, Eagle and Thunder-breeding hills would have formed the headlands of a great bay into which poured the waters of the Saskatchewans, then independent rivers, and debouching where they make the acute bends now known as their elbows."

Submergence of the continent to this extent (assuming the land to have been equally depressed on the west side) would have almost sufficed to make uninterrupted water communication, along the section exhibited, with the Pacific, or to convert the country between the McLeod Lake and Lake Stewart into a series of islands. A depression of twenty-eight hundred feet would undoubtedly have caused the formation of an estuary entered from the west by the Fraser River Valley, and connected with the eastern sea by the Peace River Gap, then a narrow rocky inlet, similar in appearance to the numerous indentations which now characterize the coast of British Columbia.

Although it may appear presumptuous on my part to speculate freely upon the age of the coal or lignite found in the eastern part of the Peace River country, yet, as the carboniferous limestone of the Rocky Mountains probably underlies that section to a great extent, the hypothesis that true coal exists within that area may be brought forward. Curiously enough, a fossil in some respects resembling the tooth of the *Holoptychius Hibberii* found by Mr. Horner in the cannel coal of Fifeshire, was found associated with the specimen of the coal to which I have referred.

www.ingramcontent.com/pod-product-compliance
Lightning Source LLC
Chambersburg PA
CBHW031351230426
43670CB00006B/506